T0027102

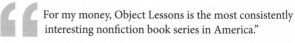

For my money, Object Lessons is the most consistently interesting nonfiction book series in America."

Megan Volpert, *PopMatters*

Besides being beautiful little hand-sized objects themselves, showcasing exceptional writing, the wonder of these books is that they exist at all . . . Uniformly excellent, engaging, thought-provoking, and informative."

Jennifer Bort Yacovissi,
Washington Independent Review of Books

. . . edifying and entertaining . . . perfect for slipping in a pocket and pulling out when life is on hold."

Sarah Murdoch, *Toronto Star*

Though short, at roughly 25,000 words apiece, these books are anything but slight."

Marina Benjamin, *New Statesman*

[W]itty, thought-provoking, and poetic . . . These little books are a page-flipper's dream."

John Timpane, *The Philadelphia Inquirer*

The joy of the series, of reading *Remote Control*, *Golf Ball*, *Driver's License*, *Drone*, *Silence*, *Glass*, *Refrigerator*, *Hotel*, and *Waste* (more titles are listed as forthcoming) in quick succession, lies in encountering the various turns through which each of their authors has been put by his or her object. As for Benjamin, so for the authors of the series, the object predominates, sits squarely center stage, directs the action. The object decides the genre, the chronology, and the limits of the study. Accordingly, the author has to take her cue from the *thing* she chose or that chose her. The result is a wonderfully uneven series of books, each one a *thing* unto itself."

Julian Yates, *Los Angeles Review of Books*

The Object Lessons series has a beautifully simple premise. Each book or essay centers on a specific object. This can be mundane or unexpected, humorous or politically timely. Whatever the subject, these descriptions reveal the rich worlds hidden under the surface of things."

Christine Ro, *Book Riot*

. . . a sensibility somewhere between Roland Barthes and Wes Anderson."

Simon Reynolds, author of *Retromania: Pop Culture's Addiction to Its Own Past*

OBJECTLESSONS

A book series about the hidden lives of ordinary things.

Series Editors:

Ian Bogost and Christopher Schaberg

Advisory Board:

Sara Ahmed, Jane Bennett, Jeffrey Jerome Cohen, Johanna
Drucker, Raiford Guins, Graham Harman, renée hoogland,
Pam Houston, Eileen Joy, Douglas Kahn, Daniel Miller,
Esther Milne, Timothy Morton, Kathleen Stewart, Nigel
Thrift, Rob Walker, Michele White

In association with

  Georgia Tech ∥ Center for Media Studies

BOOKS IN THE SERIES

blackface

AYANNA THOMPSON

BLOOMSBURY ACADEMIC
NEW YORK • LONDON • OXFORD • NEW DELHI • SYDNEY

BLOOMSBURY ACADEMIC
Bloomsbury Publishing Inc
1385 Broadway, New York, NY 10018, USA
50 Bedford Square, London, WC1B 3DP, UK
29 Earlsfort Terrace, Dublin 2, Ireland

BLOOMSBURY, BLOOMSBURY ACADEMIC and the Diana logo are
trademarks of Bloomsbury Publishing Plc

First published in the United States of America 2021

Library of Congress Cataloging-in-Publication Data
Names: Thompson, Ayanna, 1972-author.
Title: Blackface / Ayanna Thompson.
Description: New York, NY: Bloomsbury Academic, 2021. |
Series: Object lessons | Includes bibliographical references and index. |
Summary: "Investigates what blackface is, why it occurred, and
what its legacies are in the 21st century"–Provided by publisher.
Identifiers: LCCN 2020039617 | ISBN 9781501374012 (hardback) |
ISBN 9781501374029 (epub) | ISBN 9781501374036 (pdf)
Subjects: LCSH: Blackface–History. | Blackface entertainers–History. |
Blackface entertainers–United States–History. | Racism–History. |
Racism–United States–History.
Classification: LCC PN2071.B58 .T46 2021 | DDC 810.9/3556–dc23
LC record available at https://lccn.loc.gov/2020039617

ISBN: PB: 978-1-5013-7401-2
ePDF: 978-1-5013-7403-6
eBook: 978-1-5013-7402-9

Series: Object Lessons

Typeset by Deanta Global Publishing Services, Chennai, India
Printed and bound in the United States of America

To find out more about our authors and books visit www.bloomsbury.com
and sign up for our newsletters.

CONTENTS

1 WHY WRITE THIS BOOK?

When my son, Dash, was in the third grade from 2011 to 2012, he attended a private school that prided itself on its academic rigor. In fact, each eight-year-old student was required to do a year-long research project on an influential person in history. As the culmination of their research, the kids had to make a poster that highlighted their person's life and accomplishments, and then dress up as their person and answer questions as if they were the famous person during the poster presentation. It was a lot of work, and the presentations were impressive. That year there were astronauts and entertainers, politicians and athletes, humanitarians and playwrights.

And there were also several little white children in full-on blackface makeup—they were "Martin Luther King Jr.," "Serena Williams," and "Arthur Ashe." As I walked around the room, looking at the posters and interacting with the famous, historical people, I was stunned when I saw the first blacked-up child. Attempting to keep my face neutral,

I asked questions about "Martin Luther King Jr.'s" life and praised the student for her hard work. It was clear that she had immense respect and reverence for Dr. King—he was her hero. She beamed through her blacked-up face, proud to be him. I stared on in an attempt not to register my horror and dismay.

After taking this in, I immediately went to find the school's principal to ask what was happening. Was makeup allowed? Encouraged? Did the teachers facilitate this? Were the parents involved? What conversations had they had about cross-racial impersonation, even if this all occurred under the auspices of hero worship? The principal seemed not to understand what I was saying—that the children's performances were veering dangerously close to blackface. He seemed confused and indicated that he thought I was making a tempest in a teapot. I could see in his eyes that he was reading me as an irrationally angry black woman, and then he asked, "What is blackface minstrelsy anyway?"

I was gobsmacked by the question. In fact, I was quickly becoming the angry black woman he thought I was, wondering why I should have to explain American history to an American educator at a tony private school. Why didn't he know this already? Why was it my job to teach him our shared history? Why did I have to pay this black tax on top of the tuition I was already paying? I was enraged by his ignorance because it made starkly visible the inequality of our experiences. I had to know this history because it affects me and my children in the twenty-first century; he did not because of his white privilege, which was expressed through an implicit notion that this history did not, does not, and will not impact him or the white charges in his private school.

When my anger was less blinding and began to subside (I was a rationally angry black woman, after all!), I recognized that the principal's ignorance was symptomatic of the American amnesia with regard to racism and racial violence. The history is difficult, and the solutions are neither readily apparent nor easily achievable; so forgetting, while not necessarily natural, is widespread, pervasive, and common. And forgetting blackface minstrelsy—a performance tradition from the early nineteenth century—is easy to accomplish because it happened *back then* (i.e., it's over and has no resonance in today's world).

The principal's reaction, while unfair, was actually normal. But I am not content with *this* normal state of being. I need to be able to make it as impossible for him to forget as it is for me—it is both of our history after all. I need to be able to combat the extensive drift toward amnesia. This book is my attempt. This book is a defiant and material act of remembering our collective American history. This book is for every parent, teacher, friend, or colleague who has had to face and address similar questions about the uses, problems, or issues with blackface.

In order to explain what blackface is, why it occurred, and what its legacies are in the twenty-first century, I will ask repeatedly why the handful of black and brown children in my son's third-grade class did not whiten up to be "William

Shakespeare," "Sir Isaac Newton," and their other white heroes. Not one of the children of color in my son's class applied racial prosthetics to look white. Why not? Were they less committed to the fidelity of their representations? Did they know something the white children did not? Or, did the white children know something the black and brown children did not? These questions haunt this book and fuel my writing of it.

2 MEGYN KELLY, JUSTIN TRUDEAU, OR (FILL IN ANOTHER PUBLIC FIGURE'S NAME)

In order to explain what blackface is, I begin with several examples from recent history. In fact, the four examples detailed below all occurred within the scope of one year—from October 2018 to September 2019. I quote extensively from the individuals involved because part of what propels the use of blackface is white people's belief in their white innocence. When defending, explaining, and even apologizing for the employment of blackface, white people rely on the logic and rhetoric of their innocence. In fact, they frame blackface as either an act of celebration and love, or as an act of imitation and verisimilitude. The logic of white innocence unites the actions of the disparate public figures who have engaged in blackface as adults, and it also unites their defenses of their actions. Despite their various political stances, their actions are yoked together by the inherent white supremacist logic of white innocence.

Example #1: On the October 23, 2018, show *Megyn Kelly Today* (NBC, episode 212), Megyn Kelly, Melissa Rivers, Jenna Bush Hager, and Jacob Soboroff discussed controversial Halloween costumes on a segment entitled "Halloween Costume Crackdown." Kelly began the segment by declaring that political correctness had gone too far. She reported that Kent University in the UK had issued a warning to its students not to wear controversial Halloween costumes. When her interlocutors indicated that they thought this was reasonable to ensure that the students did not offend others (a Nazi costume was roundly denounced as offensive and inexcusable), Kelly was both perplexed and annoyed. She responded:

> But what is racist? You get in trouble if you are a white person who puts on blackface for Halloween, or if you are a black person who puts on whiteface for Halloween. Back when I was a kid that was okay as long as you were dressing up as, like, a character. . . . There was a controversy on the *Real Housewives of New York* with Luann [de Lesseps] as she dressed up as Diana Ross and she made her skin look darker than it really is. And people said that that was racist. And I don't know, I felt like who doesn't love Diana Ross? She wants to look like Diana Ross for one day. I don't know how that got racist on Halloween. It's not like

she's walking around like that in general. . . . I can't keep up with the number of people we are offending by just being, like, normal people.[1]

Kelly's statement in support of the use of blackface on Halloween relies on both the assumed innocence of a desire for verisimilitude ("Back when I was a kid [blackface] was okay as long as you were dressing up as like a character") and the assumed innocence of a desire to celebrate others ("who doesn't love Diana Ross? She wants to look like Diana Ross for one day"). And the logic and rhetoric of her position ends with an explicit appeal to white innocence ("I can't keep up with the number of people we are offending by just being like normal people"). She is "normal people," and her intentions should seem that way too, even if she were to apply blackface for Halloween (Figure 2.1).

Kelly was immediately criticized by her colleagues and viewers. Don Lemon, a black journalist, took direct aim at Kelly's claims to white innocence. In an interview on CNN, Lemon said to Chris Cuomo, "Megyn is 47 years old—she's our age. There has never been a time in that 47 years that blackface has been acceptable."[2] Countering her claim that it was acceptable "back then" when there was no political correctness, Lemon reminds his audience that "back then" was the 1980s, not the 1880s. Kelly subsequently released a written apology and had an on-air discussion with people of color about cross-racial dressing. Nonetheless, NBC canceled her show the following day. At the time of writing this book,

FIGURE 2.1 In 2018, Megyn Kelly defended Luann de Lesseps "Diana Ross" costume by saying, "Who doesn't love Diana Ross?" Twitter.

however, Megyn Kelly seems poised to make a comeback to television.

Example #2: Three months later on January 24, 2019, *The Tallahassee Democrat*, a local newspaper in Florida, released photos of Michael Ertel, Florida's secretary of state. Ertel, who had served as the chief elections officer in Seminole County for fourteen years, had been appointed by Florida's republican governor, Ron DeSantis, only a few weeks earlier in December 2018. The photo was from a 2005 Halloween party in which he appeared to be cross-dressed and blackfaced (Figure 2.2). Wearing a New Orleans Saints

FIGURE 2.2 In 2005, Michael Ertel, then the Seminole County supervisor of elections, donned blackface to portray a Hurricane Katrina victim at a Halloween party. Twitter.

bandana, earrings, and large fake breasts under a blue T-shirt with the handwritten slogan "Katrina Victim," Ertel appears in the 2005 image to be mocking the victims of Hurricane Katrina, the Category Five tropical cyclone that devastated New Orleans only two months earlier in August 2005. Hurricane Katrina caused numerous deaths, $125 billion in damages, and displaced one million residents.

Is it possible that Ertel felt he was honoring the victims through his Halloween costume? Was his costume an homage to the victims' resiliency and style in the face of devastation? It's conceivable, and we may never know. *The Miami Herald* reports: "In his resignation email, Ertel made no reference to the controversy that ended his brief term. His email signature quoted Abraham Lincoln: 'These men ask for just the same thing, fairness, and fairness only. This, so far as in my power, they, and all others, shall have.'"[3] While Ertel did not issue an explicit statement about his motives for creating and wearing his Halloween costume, his email signature quotation does rely on the logic of white innocence. His plea for fairness in the quotation from Abraham Lincoln—the American president who freed the enslaved in the Emancipation Proclamation— seems to indicate a belief in his own sense of morality and justice. Is it fair to force him to resign his office over a Halloween costume, the email signature quotation seems to be asking?

Example #3: Exactly eight days later, on February 1, 2019, the conservative website Big League Politics was the first media outlet to post images from Ralph Northam's medical school yearbook (Figure 2.3). The democratic governor

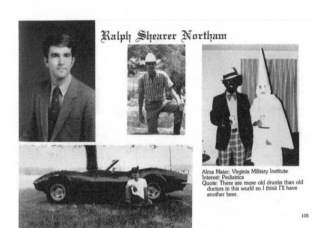

Ralph Shearer Northam

Alma Mater: Virginia Military Institute
Interest: Pediatrics
Quote: There are more old drunks than old
doctors in this world so I think I'll have
another beer.

105

FIGURE 2.3 Ralph Northam's 1984 Eastern Virginia Medical School yearbook page includes an image of blackface.

of Virginia, who had assumed his office in January 2018, graduated from Eastern Virginia Medical School in Norfolk, Virginia in 1984. His yearbook page contains four images: one a standard, posed school photo of him in a suit; one of him in a cowboy hat, holding a Budweiser beer can; one of him in a baseball cap sitting in front of a convertible; and one of two people both holding beer cans—one in blackface and one in a white Ku Klux Klan robe and hood. Governor Northam apologized immediately, saying "I am deeply sorry for the decision I made to appear as I did in this photo and for the hurt that decision caused then and now. This behavior is not in keeping with who I am today."[4]

Unlike Ertel, however, Northam resisted the calls for his resignation, and by the next day (February 2, 2019) his memory had been clarified about his appearance in blackface. In a press conference, Northam explained:

In the hours since I made my statement yesterday, I reflected with my family and classmates from the time and affirmed my conclusion that I am not the person in that photo. While I did not appear in this photo, I am not surprised by its appearance in the EVMS yearbook. In the place and time where I grew up, many actions that we rightfully recognize as abhorrent today were commonplace. My belief that I did not wear that costume or attend that party stems in part from my clear memory of other mistakes I made in the same period of my life. That same year, I did participate in a dance contest in San Antonio in which I darkened my face as part of a Michael Jackson costume. I look back now and regret that I did not understand the harmful legacy of an action like that. It is because my memory of that action is so vivid that I truly do not believe that I am in the picture of my yearbook. You remember these things.[5]

While Northam's rhetoric, unlike Megyn Kelly's or Michael Ertel's, was apologetic, it still rested on the same belief in his white innocence ("I did not understand the harmful legacy of an action like that"). He even went on to explain that there was a critical difference between the yearbook photo, which was "offensive" and "racist," and his made-up appearance as Michael Jackson at the dance contest, because: (a) it was a product of his time ("In the place and time where I grew up, many actions that we rightfully recognize as abhorrent today were commonplace") and (b) it was an act of celebration performed in ignorance of its historical implications.

A reporter at the February 2, 2019, press conference asked, "Governor, at the San Antonio party you said you darkened your face. I just want to be perfectly clear, were you in blackface?" And Governor Northam elaborated, "I wasn't. I mean, I'll tell you exactly what I did, Alan. I dressed up as . . . Michael Jackson. I had the shoes. I had the glove, and I used just a little bit of shoe polish to put on my cheeks. And the reason I used a very little bit is because—I don't know if anybody has ever tried that—but you cannot get shoe polish off. But it was a dance contest. I had always liked Michael Jackson. I actually won the contest because I had learned how to do the moonwalk." When he was asked by a reporter if he could still moonwalk, the governor looked around to see if there was enough room to perform his moves next to the podium. Then the governor's wife saliently warned him, "inappropriate circumstances." The governor clearly wanted to explain and demonstrate his love for Michael Jackson. He can still do Jackson's signature dance move. That is a sign of deep admiration and love, and an indication of his white innocence, right?

The governor went on to say that a black staffer had recently explained to him why it was offensive to black up to perform as Michael Jackson. At the very end of the press conference another reporter asked, "Do you think it is problematic that you need to have it explained to you that blackface is offensive?" Attempting to leave the podium, Governor Northam responded, "No. You know, I'm not a person of color. And people of color experience different things. It affects them in different ways." Like the principal at my son's private elementary school, Governor Northam's logic stemmed from a belief that ignorance is a type of innocence. Despite the fact that he is a highly educated *doctor*, his sense of American history is experienced "in different ways" from people of color. And the implied message is that there is no fault in that.

Thinking that the governor would resign, reporters began investigating the succession chain in Virginia. As this happened, the lieutenant governor, the next in line, became embroiled in a sexual harassment scandal. The next in line after the lieutenant governor is the attorney general of the state. Immediately after the governor's press conference cited above, Virginia's attorney general, Mark Herring, called for Northam to resign: "It is no longer possible for Governor Northam to lead our Commonwealth and it is time for him to step down." Unfortunately, for the attorney general, it was revealed that he too had appeared in blackface at a college party in the 1980s. Five days later he admitted, "In 1980, when I was a 19-year-old undergraduate in college [at the University of Virginia], some friends suggested we attend a party dressed like rappers we listened to at the time, like Kurtis Blow, and perform a song . . . we dressed up and put on wigs and brown makeup."[6] Despite the fact that the attorney general thought that the governor should resign, he employed the exact same logic of white innocence for his own defense. He dressed in blackface with his friends because they liked rappers like Kurtis Blow. At the time of writing this (May 2020), the governor, lieutenant governor, and attorney general of Virginia all still have their offices. *Oh! Hush! Virginny . . .*

Example #4: Then came Justin Trudeau. On September 18, 2019, *Time Magazine* released a story about the liberal leader of Canada, Justin Trudeau, appearing in blackface at a 2001 school fundraiser themed "Arabian Nights." Trudeau was a teacher at the West Point Grey Academy at the time, and he went to the school's fundraiser dressed as "Aladdin" (Figure 2.4). When the prime minister was asked if this was the only time he had blacked up, he told the CBC News reporter David Cochrane that "there was one other incident, dating from when he was in a high school talent show at Montreal's Collège Jean-de-Brébeuf. He wore blackface to sing Harry Belafonte's hit 'Day O (Banana Boat Song).'"[7] But on the following day (September 19, 2019), yet another image of Trudeau was published—this one from a party in the 1990s.

In his first press conference on the matter, Trudeau apologized profusely, but he also repeated (three times) that his actions were done out of ignorance: "I should have known better then, but I didn't."[8] This rhetoric, as we have seen from the previous examples, stems from the logic of white innocence. The following day (September 19, 2019), Trudeau held another press conference and his rhetoric shifted slightly.

FIGURE 2.4 West Point Grey Academy's April 2001 newsletter featured this image of Justin Trudeau as "Aladdin" in blackface.

While he still maintained the logic of white innocence—"I didn't understand how hurtful this is to people who live with discrimination every day"; "I should have understood that then"; and "I'm not that person anymore"—he explicitly tied his past ignorance to his white privilege. In fact, Trudeau talked about his "privilege" five times in the course of this one press conference.

Then Trudeau went on to use the rhetoric that underpins critical race theory to demonstrate his movement from being privileged to becoming an "ally":

I am certainly conscious that in my political career, as leader and indeed as prime minister, we've taken many concrete actions to fight against racism, to fight against intolerance, to fight against anti-black racism specifically, to recognize unconscious bias, [and the] systemic discrimination that exists in Canada and elsewhere, to work to overcome and to recognize [the] intersectionalities that people live with in a way that so many of us cannot understand or appreciate, the micro-aggressions and the challenges being faced [because of them]. And so even though we have moved forward in significant ways as a government, what I did, the choices I made, hurt people, hurt people who thought I was an ally. I am an ally, but this is something I deeply regret, and I never should have done.[9]

When I first heard the above statement, I was stunned by Trudeau's use of very specific critical race theory discourse. It was almost as if Trudeau, literally, took a page out of Kimberlé Crenshaw's book, *On Intersectionality*.[10] The function of the specificity, however, is not only to signal that Trudeau is a knowledgeable ally, but also to signal that he is completely different from the person who applied blackface eighteen years prior (and twenty years prior, and twenty-five years prior, and . . .). He was ignorant and innocent, but he has been educated and now has an even purer heart. While I believe Trudeau's knowledge and prefer it to Northam's seeming continued ignorance ("Do you think it is problematic that you need to have it explained to you that blackface is offensive?" "No."), I distrust the logic behind them both precisely because they rely on a belief in white innocence.

The reason I distrust that logic is because it seems as if it is a state—innocence—that is the sole domain of white people. Is it possible for black and brown Americans to be framed as innocent even when ignorant? This question holds a lot of weight in the current social moment when unarmed black men and women are being killed by police officers in alarmingly frequent rates. Why aren't unarmed black men, women, and children (I'm thinking of the numerous black teenagers killed by police officers too) viewed as innocent?

But perhaps I should ask an easier question first: Why don't black children apply whiteface during Halloween? Despite Megyn Kelly's assertion that "You get in trouble if . . . you are a black person who puts on whiteface for Halloween," whiteface is not a widespread phenomenon on Halloween. While Northam (as Michael Jackson), Herring (as Kurtis Blow), and Trudeau (as Harry Belafonte) claimed to be dressing up as singers whom they admired as teenagers, when I was a teenager, I really liked white singers like Debbie Harry, Alison Moyet, and Annie Lennox, but I never thought to celebrate my love for them by whitening my face. Singing along, yes; whitening up, no! Why is this the case? Are we not innocent enough?

3 WHAT IS BLACKFACE?

Perhaps now is a good moment to take a step back to explain blackface more fully. What exactly is *blackface*? On the most basic level, blackface is the application of any prosthetic—makeup, soot, burnt cork, minerals, masks, etc.—to imitate the complexion of another race. While some people distinguish between blackface and brownface to separate impersonations of blackness from Indian-ness, Hispanic-ness, etc., I will address them together as being united by a desire to perform as, or appear to be, another race.

In performance, the application of black makeup dates back to at least the medieval period when guild records show that some of the devils in religious dramas were portrayed as being black. Anthony Barthelemy explains, "In many medieval miracle plays, the souls of the damned were represented by actors painted black or in black costumes. However, the prevalence of the tradition can be clearly seen in the mystery plays. In the play of the Fall in the Towneley, York, Coventry, and Chester cycles, Lucifer and his confederate rebels, after having sinned, turn black."[1] It looks as if natural oils like bitumen, soot from coal, and black clothes were used to convey the blackness of the fallen angels in these medieval guild performances of biblical narratives.

In Shakespeare's lifetime, there were numerous theatrical Moors, Africans, and Turks who were portrayed by white actors in various types of racial prosthetics; the theaters used costuming, wigs and beards, makeup, masks, and even fake noses to convey racial difference. In fact, the only contemporary drawing we have from a Shakespeare performance includes a "Moor" (Figure 3.1). We believe that Henry Peacham went to see a performance of Shakespeare's first tragedy, *Titus Andronicus*, in 1595 and then went home and memorialized his experience by drawing some of the characters and writing out bits of dialogue from the play. Aaron the Moor, one of the villains in the play, looks as if he was performed by a white actor in blackface makeup, a black afro wig (affixed with a headband), and either black stockings and gloves or more makeup that covered the actor's hands and legs. One scholar tabulates that between 1579 and 1642 there were at least fifty plays with racialized figures, and another scholar counts at least seventy productions with black characters.[2] The Renaissance theaters, then, had to have been flush in racial prosthetics!

This performance tradition—of white men applying and employing racial prosthetics to perform as black characters— hopped the pond to the American colonies in the late eighteenth century. *Othello* was one of the most popular

FIGURE 3.1 The Peacham Drawing, or the Longleat manuscript, dates from 1595 and is thought to be the only surviving contemporary Shakespearean illustration. The drawing of Aaron the Moor provides some clues about how blackness was performed on the early modern stage. The Marquess of Bath, Longleat.

plays on the early American stage, but there were various other popular plays that contained black characters who were portrayed by white male actors. The plays that included black characters ranged generically from tragedies like Thomas Morton's *The Slave* (1816), to comedies like Isaac Bickerstaff's *The Padlock* (1768), to pantomimes like John Fawcett's *Obi; or, Three Finger'd Jack* (1800), to equestrian dramas like John Fawcett's *The Secret Mine* (1812), to comic operas like George Colman's *Inkle and Yarico* (1787). The performance of blackness in the Western world, then, was from the start a white endeavor. To be a black character onstage was to be performed by a white actor in racial prosthetics.

Blackface minstrelsy is a specific performance mode and genre that developed in the early nineteenth century. With characters with names like Jim Crow, Zip Coon, and Mammy, these performances were comprised of skits, monologues, songs, and dances that supposedly imitated enslaved persons or recently freed enslaved persons. The genre was comedically based and was performed by white men: when there were female characters, the male performers were both blacked up and cross-dressed. While the earliest minstrel performances were done as one-man shows, after the Civil War minstrel troupes were formed and transformed the mode into a larger, performance extravaganza. The mode and genre were so popular that there were active minstrel troupes well into the mid- to late-twentieth century. "The Black and White Minstrel Show," for instance, ran on BBC1 television in the UK until its cancelation in 1978. To be clear, that's *not* 1878!

When public figures like Governor Ralph Northam and Prime Minister Justin Trudeau are outed for applying blackface, they are often criticized for either tapping into, or being insensitive to, the history of blackface minstrelsy. These public figures often deny that they are citing this tradition. In an attempt to distance and distinguish their actions from blackface minstrelsy, they will claim that their use of blackface was done in a celebratory manner (remember, for the love of Michael Jackson, Kurtis Blow, Harry Belafonte, and Diana Ross). Yet, the logic and rhetoric behind blackface minstrelsy itself is that it is either an imitative act or celebratory act.

Will it surprise you to learn that the early nineteenth-century originators of blackface minstrelsy claimed their performances were both imitative in an ethnographic way and celebratory of black culture? While Thomas Dartmouth (T. D./Daddy) Rice (1808–60, b. New York) is often called the "father of American minstrelsy," the performance mode, techniques, and genre that cohered into the first extant playbill for the "jumping of Jim Crow" (September 22, 1830, in Louisville, Kentucky) were being explored by many American *and* English actors.[3]

For instance, the English comedian and imitator, Charles Mathews (1776–1835, b. Devon), influenced Rice significantly. Mathews became famous for his At Home performances, a type of one-man show in which he imitated different people with different accents from different walks of life (e.g., Scottish women, Parisienne sophisticates, English men and women with Cockney accents). He toured the United States in 1822 hoping to find material for a new show based on American oddities. Writing to his friend James Smith on February 23, 1823, Mathews worried that he would not have enough material for a new show because "There is such a universal sameness of manner and character, so uniform a style of walking and looking, of dressing and thinking" that it wouldn't be funny.[4] Where was the variety in America, he worried?

Adept at spinning a good yarn, Mathews built up the suspense in his letter to Smith to reveal that he had found some surprisingly good material—"specimens" of "black gentry."[5] Mathews crowed to Smith:

I shall be rich in black fun. I have studied their broken English carefully. It is pronounced the real thing, even by the Yankees. It is a pity that I dare not touch upon the preacher. I know its danger, but perhaps the absurdity might give a *colour* to it—a *black* Methodist! I have a specimen from life, which is relished highly in private. A *leetle* bit you shall have. By the by, they call the nigger meetings *"Black Brimstone Churches."* "My wordy bredrin, it a no use to come to de meetum-house to ear de most hellygunt orashions if a no puts de *cent* into de plate; de spiritable man cannot get a on widout de temporalities; twelve 'postles must hab de candle to burn. You dress a self up in de fine blue a cot, and a bandalore breechum, and tink a look like a gemman, but no more like a gemman dan put a finger in de fire, and take him out again, widout you put a de money in a de plate. He lend a to de poor, lend to de Law (Lord), if you like a de secoority drop a de cents in to de box. My sister in a de gallery too dress em up wid de poke a de bonnet, and de furbellow-tippet, and look in de glass and say, 'Pretty Miss Phyllis, how bell I look!' but no pretty in de eye of the Law (Lord) widout a drop a cent in de plate. My friend and bredren, in my endeavour to save you, I come across de bay in de stim a boat. I never was more shock dan when I see de race a horse a rubbin down. No fear o' de Law afore dere eye on de Sabbat a day, ben I was tinking of de great enjawment my friend at a Baltimore was to have dis night, dey rub a down a horse for de use of de debbil. Twix you and I, no see what de white folk make so much fun of us, for when dey act so foolish demselve, dey tink dey know ebery ting, and dat we poor brack people know noting at all amose (almost). Den shew dem how much more dollars you can put in de plate dan de white meetum-houses. But, am sorry to say, some of you put three cent in a plate, and take a out a quarter a dollar. What de say ven you go to hebben? Dey ask you what you do wid de twenty-two cent you take out of de plate when you put in de tree cent? What you go do den?"[6]

I have quoted from Mathews's letter at length because it is evidence of how much time and energy he put into claiming that he has studied black Americans' "broken English." He even uses scientific language to claim that he has copied a specific "specimen," a black preacher. He brags that white Americans, "the Yankees," praise his verisimilitude ("It is pronounced the real thing"). And he notes that while he won't be able to make fun of the black preacher in his public performances, he will include a "*leetle* bit" for his pen pal. In other words, Mathews frames his interest in this new material as an ethnographer would. He has studied and reproduced what he has heard—at least that is what he claimed . . .

By March 25, 1824 Mathews debuted his new one-man show, *A Trip to America*, in which he performed the new material he had gathered in the United States, including the following skit and song about his supposed visits to the "Niggers Theatre":

> I take the opportunity of visiting the Niggers Theatre. The black population being, in the national theatres, under certain restrictions, have, to be quite at their ease, a theatre of their own. Here I see a black tragedian (the Kentucky Roscius) perform the character of Hamlet
>
> > To-*by*, or not to-*by*, dat is de question,
> > Wedder it be noble in de *head*, to suffer
> > De *tumps* and *bumps* of de outrageous fortune,
> > Or to take up de arms against a sea of *hubble bubble*,
> > And by *opossum*, end 'em.
>
> No sooner had he said the "*opossum*," which he meant for "oppose them," than a universal cry of "Opossum! Opossum! Song! Song!" ran through the sable auditory. This, I learnt from a Kentucky planter, was a great favourite with the negroes, and a genu-*ine* melody. I was informed that "Opossum up a Gum Tree" was a national air, a sort of "God save the King" of the negroes, and that being reminded of it by Hamlet's pronunciation of "oppose 'em," there was no doubt but that they would have it sung.[7]

Mathews then performed the song he said he heard at the "Nigger's Theatre." His approach, then, was to present his performance as if it were witnessed, recorded on paper, and then practiced and reproduced for his London audience so that they too could feel as if they went on a trip to America. The logic behind this early cross-racial impersonation is that it is not scripted—that is, it is not fictional or fantastical—but rather recorded—that is, it is truthful and compelled by a desire for verisimilitude.

It is important to note that the performance Mathews claims to have seen at the "Nigger's Theatre" *did not occur*—the African Theatre, which I will describe in the next chapter—never performed *Hamlet*, the lead actor was not from Kentucky, and they never sang "Opossum up a Gum Tree," a song of dubious origins. In other words, the performance, which was touted as being a faithful reproduction of events experienced by Mathews firsthand, was in reality a fiction scripted by a talented performer and promoter. Part of the legacy of blackface performances stems from this false claim of reverence through faithful reproduction.

While it is unclear if Mathews used the aid of racial prosthetics, his audiences often recalled his performances as if he had been physically transformed. There are several artistic sketches from *A Trip to America* that depict his black characters as looking black, and friends commented on his ability to shape-shift. One noted, for example, that "Mathews, the mimic, could effect so extraordinary a change in the appearance and expression of his face, by simply [t]ying up the tip of his nose with a piece of catgut" that he could trick his "intimate friends" to such an extent that "not one of them . . . recognized him."[8] Again, Mathews trafficked in protean changes which he often claimed were based on verisimilitude. And, in turn, his audiences praised his work for being so real that they saw his blackness *even when no racial prosthetics were employed.*

T. D. Rice also capitalized on the popularity of several other comic, cross-racial performances of black identity when he began Jumping Jim Crow in 1830. The other major hit that influenced Rice was *Tom and Jerry, or, Life in London* by William Thomas Moncrieff and based on Pierce Egan's *Life in London* (1821). The play related the adventures of the country bumpkin Jerry, who visited his learned cousin Tom in London. They traveled through various parts of the city with Tom's witty urbanite friend Logic, encountering different types of city dwellers, and get into various types of city trouble (gambling, incarceration, etc.). Because the play offered a type of tour of London, the script contained dialogue in various different vernaculars, including two for "black" characters. One black character was "African Sal," a black woman who made an appearance toward the end of the play in a bar. Her speech attempted to imitate a drunken black vernacular. This role, however, was performed by white male actors who were cross-dressed and blacked up.

The second black character was "Billy Waters," who was an actual enslaved black American (1778–1823, b. US) who is thought to have traded his servitude to work as a British sailor. Waters played the violin outside the Adelphi Theatre and cut a striking figure because he wore a British sailing uniform and had a peg leg. There were several contemporary portraits of Waters, celebrating his fame as a street performer, including one from 1822 that is labeled "The notorious Billy Black 'At Home' to a London Street Party," which showed him performing for a crowd on the street (Figure 3.2). Adding a touch of the real, *Tom and Jerry* included city scenes with actual street performers. In the original script for *Tom and Jerry*, Billy Waters had lines specifically designated for him. Thus, *Tom and Jerry, or, Life in London* attempted to capitalize

FIGURE 3.2 An early black American performer, Billy Waters is thought to have traded his enslavement to be a British sailor. He became famous for performing the violin on the streets of London. "The notorious Billy Black 'At Home' to a London Street Party" (1822). The Wellcome Collection (CC by 4.0).

on the desire for verisimilitude and authenticity by including two black characters.

But once again we must interrogate the realness of this performance. For one thing, Billy Waters died in 1823 even though his character continued to be performed in the immensely popular *Tom and Jerry* for years. Were there other black street performers who worked under the name "Billy Waters"? Or, was his role transformed into a blackface one? The "Billy Waters" character was removed from the New York adaptions that began in 1823; only the crossed-dressed and blacked up "African Sal" survived. Nonetheless, the rhetoric of authenticity survived—you can experience a tour of the real London with this play.

T. D. Rice was influenced not only by the performance modes of Mathews's *A Trip to America* and Moncrieff's *Tom and Jerry*, but also by the rhetoric that bolstered the logic behind them. He was instrumental in making the blackface minstrel mode an identifiable and coherent comedic tradition that had immense commercial appeal. He claimed that his earliest performances as "Jim Crow" were an impersonation of an actual enslaved person he witnessed singing and dancing on hobbled legs. Edmon S. Conner, an actor with whom Rice worked in a summer touring company, reported to the *New York Times* in 1881:

> [In] back of the theatre [in Louisville, Kentucky] was a livery-stable kept by a man named Crow. The actors could look into the stable yard from the theatre, and were

particularly amused by an old decrepit negro, who used to do odd jobs for Crow. As was then usual with slaves, they called themselves after their owner, so that old Daddy had assumed the name of Jim Crow. He was very much deformed, the right shoulder being drawn high up, the left leg stiff and crooked at the knee, giving him a painful, but at the same time, laughable limp. He used to croon a queer old tune with words of his own, and at the end of each verse would give a little jump, and when he came down he set his "heel a-rockin'" . . . Rice watched him closely and saw the hero was a character unknown to the stage. He wrote several verses, changed the air somewhat quickened it a good deal, made up exactly like Daddy, and sang it to a Louisville audience. They were wild with delight, and on the first night he was recalled twenty times.[9]

As must be clear, I think the veracity of this narrative is less important than its employment of blackface's consistent exculpatory fiction—that the performance genre is based on replicating real life.

While this "origin" story for Jumping Jim Crow was challenged by several of Rice's contemporaries, Rice doubled down on the ethnographic foundations of blackface minstrelsy. Jim Crow was an enslaved figure, but Rice went on to expand his repertoire to create characters he claimed were based on recently freed persons—black dandies. While "dandy" was a term that was initially used to describe a white man who dressed in high fashion, the black dandy was assumed to ape or imitate high fashion foolishly.

When Rice debuted *Oh! Hush!*, a play that featured a black dandy named "Gumbo Cuff," to sellout audiences in New York, "Colonel" George Pope Morris wrote an article attacking Rice. He warned his readers that although "Gumbo Cuff is one of those finely tempered, susceptible beings, which Shakespeare in his 'Othello' . . . must have conceived. Let no one, however, suppose that Mr. Rice has taken a thing from Shakespeare."[10] The black dandy, Morris feared, was too compelling and might trick "New York Desdemonas." T. D. Rice retorted in terms that should be very familiar by now. He wrote:

I have merely sought to give a sketch of the lowest classes, something in the same style with *Tom and Jerry*, so long the favorite of the stage in England as well as in America; which, I am told by those who have traveled, is itself imitated from a style of humble life drama, exceedingly popular even among the audiences more fastidious in their tastes, of other countries. I assure the public that my object in doing this, was to emulate my friend and their favorite the Colonel [the author of the complaint], and hold the Mirror up to nature . . .

I am sorry that the nigger affectation of white manners should be so annoying to the *Mirror*; but there was a precedent for this sort of "high life below stairs" in the farce of that name, which was famous even before

Colonel Pluck was ever heard of. And I do not see why Colonel Pluck should be so anxious to warn the New York Desdemonas against Gumbo Cliff, by repeating them, over and over again, that neither Gumbo Cliff nor Jim Crow are equal to Othello . . . and if dandyism is rendered contemptible in their eyes by its copying the blacks, may not the copy render a service to society by inducing the ladies to discourage its original in whites? This is the moral benefit of all caricatures, of which Gumbo Cuff puts in his claim for a share.[11]

Rice's defense of his blackface performance not only quotes from Shakespeare, but also is very specific in its performance genealogy. Rice sees minstrelsy as a natural outgrowth of *Tom and Jerry, or, Life in London*, which itself was indebted to what he labels "humble life dramas" like Charles Mathews's At Home sketches. For Rice, the minstrel show genre is in line with other popular performance modes that imitate real life.

The strange twist at the end, however, is that Rice defends this performance mode as one that should also hold the mirror up to white culture. If black dandies are offensive and potentially dangerous to New York Desdemonas, then perhaps white dandies should alter their behavior too. For Rice, blacking up to imitate black dandies is the perfect way to expose how black dandies are imitating white affectations. While Mathews's At Home sketches and Moncrieff's *Tom and Jerry* offered tours of different slices of life, Rice says that his blackface minstrel show is both imitative and instructive.

Blackface, then, is any performance in which white actors apply a racial prosthetic to perform as another race. Blackface minstrelsy is a specific comedic performance tradition that, according to its own logic, imitates, celebrates, and mocks the actions of black Americans. While both performance modes are largely regarded as offensive in the twenty-first century, blackface minstrelsy is the one that is clearly beyond the pale (pardon the pun!). Today, white actors are dissuaded from playing Othello in black makeup, but white actors are drummed out of town if they perform blackface minstrel shows.

Public figures like Megyn Kelly and Justin Trudeau are criticized for being insensitive to, and/or ignorant of, the performance history of blackface minstrelsy in particular. But can the same be said of the young children in my son's school these ten years ago? Is it fair to lump together the actions of these adult public figures with the white children who blacked up to present their research projects? Obviously, the desire of the third graders to look like MLK or Serena Williams was actually innocent, right? Obviously, their actions are different from Ralph Northam's, right? Actually, no, not so much. But to explain why this is the case, I'll need to explain the longer historical arc that led to the creation of blackface minstrelsy.

4 WHY DOES BLACKFACE EXIST?

BECAUSE OF UPPITY NEGROS, OF COURSE!

As I noted in the previous chapter, long before blackface minstrelsy jumped onto the American stage (and then swam across the oceans of the world like an invasive species), there were numerous examples of characters of color written to be performed by white actors in racial prosthetics. One must understand the history of performing blackness in earlier periods to understand how black minstrelsy came into being.

In the past, it was common for scholars to argue that Shakespeare would not have known any blacks or Jews. Now we believe that Shakespeare probably did have encounters with people of other races, ethnicities, and religions because London was a diverse landscape that reflected England's desire to be one of the major centers of trade. Shakespeare's theatrical creations were probably both a mixture of firsthand experiences with the diverse peoples passing through London and clever reimaginings of them. This mixture gets reflected in the plays he wrote for his theater—the aptly named Globe—a space that announced itself as being interested in the wider world.

England's engagement in global trade routes dramatically expanded in the sixteenth and seventeenth centuries. That meant that English travelers were experiencing new people abroad, and that non-English people were traveling to, and sometimes living in, England as well. In fact, archival work by scholars like Imtiaz Habib has shown that Shakespeare's London was much more diverse than scholars had previously understood it to be. Habib documents the numerous blacks—African, American, and Indian—living and working in sixteenth- and seventeenth-century England.[1]

Writing about the performance modes available in Shakespeare's time, Dympna Callaghan has argued that there were "two distinct, though connected, systems of representation crucially at work in the culture's preoccupation with racial others and singularly constitutive of its articulation of racial difference: the display of black people themselves (exhibition) and the simulation of negritude (mimesis)."[2] In other words, the performance of blackness occurred both through the exhibition of black and brown bodies (both alive and dead) and the imitation of blackness on theatrical stages. I will linger on this for a bit because I think it has direct bearing on the development of blackface minstrelsy.

Exhibition: Noting the numerous black servants (or enslaved persons) who were exhibited at court, Callaghan argues that the early modern English aristocracy (at the very least) enjoyed experiencing black bodies in an exhibition mode. Shakespeare makes it clear in *The Tempest* that exhibiting foreign bodies was a form of English entertainment that was enjoyed by many. One of the characters, calling Caliban a "fish," notes:

Were I in England now, as once
I was, and had but this fish painted, not a holiday
fool there but would give a piece of silver . . .
. . .
When they will not give a doit [a small coin] to
relieve a lame beggar, they will lay out ten to see a
dead Indian.

(TEMPEST 2.2.28-34)

In other words, this character notes the popularity of seeing exhibited foreign, racialized bodies in early modern England. Someone can even make money by exhibiting the corpse of a "dead Indian." Likewise, Africans were prized and valued status symbols, who were often employed to celebrate the birth of royalty. For example, there was a black trumpeter named John Blanke/Blak in the courts of Henry VII and Henry VIII. Blanke/Blak is even pictured in the Westminster Tournament Roll that depicts the 1511 celebration of Henry VIII's male heir with Catherine of Aragon ("The Little Prince Hal" died weeks later) (Figure 4.1).

FIGURE 4.1 The 1511 Westminster Tournament Roll features an image of John Blanke/Blak, a black trumpeter who worked in the courts of Henry VII and Henry VIII. *College of Arms MS Westminster Tournament Roll, 1511, membrane 28.* Reproduced by permission of the Corporation of the Kings, Heralds and Pursuivants of Arms.

At the christening of King James's first son in 1594 in Scotland, an enslaved man in gold chains pulled in a "triumphal chariot" that was twelve feet by seven feet. "It appeared to be drawne in, onely by the strength of the Moor, which was very richly attired; his traces were great chaines of pure gold." And on this triumphal chariot was "a sumptuous covered table, decked with all sorts of exquisite delicates and dainties, of patisserie, fruitages, and confections."[3] The richness of the court, then, was symbolized by the sumptuousness of the foods presented *and* by the luxuriousness of the Moor in golden chains who pulled the food in for the court. Similarly, in numerous paintings of the aristocracy from the time period, black servants/enslaved persons are featured often to highlight the beauty and luminosity of their white employer/enslavers. Whiteness looks more beautiful, rich, and luminous when placed in juxtaposition with the small, poor, and dullness of black servitude.

Mimesis: Renaissance theatres purchased and used many racial prosthetics because cross-racial performances were extremely popular. There were probably somewhere between fifty and seventy plays that contained characters of color in Shakespeare's era. White men were blacking up with great frequency in this time period, and some Renaissance actors achieved fame from these cross-racial impersonations. Edward Alleyn, for instance, is considered to be one of the first "stars" of the early modern stage, and he starred in several of the first cross-racial hits: *Tamburlaine*, *The Jew of Malta*, and *The Battle of Alcazar*. Thomas Heywood even praised Alleyn for being a "Proteus for Shapes," which when used for nineteenth-century actors like Charles Mathews, seems to be a very specific code for praising cross-racial impersonation.[4] Alleyn's primary acting rival, Richard Burbage, starred in many of Shakespeare's biggest plays including *Othello*, and he too was often praised for making the "Grieved Moor" seem real.[5]

I have highlighted this 400-year-old performance history because the two performance modes for blackness—exhibition and mimesis—remained in effect for hundreds of years in both England and America. This legacy meant that white male actors were valued for being "Protean," a shape-shifting actor who could take on different identities and races. The performance of blackness was from the start a white endeavor. To be a black character onstage was to be performed by a white actor in racial prosthetics.

Yet, the second part of this legacy is even more distressing. The legacy of early modern performance modes meant that black people were primarily valued for exhibiting their bodies. As must be clear, this is not a position of power, control, or authority. Exhibition, in fact, disempowers the person on display because all of the power resides with the viewer. Think about it: No one is praised for their skill or prowess at exhibiting themselves. Rather, the bodies on display are praised for being amazing specimens, natural wonders, and/or remarkable examples of God's handiwork. In other words, the people on display are not credited with making themselves; they are viewed as passive, and either Nature or God is credited with the act of making.

But what does this have to do with blackface minstrelsy, you might ask? There were a few black actors who seem to have noted this performance conundrum in which being black meant that one was never read, assessed, or valued for being talented or skilled. These few black actors attempted to appropriate the power of crossing over to be valued as a "Proteus of Shapes." The threat that these attempts at black-performed cross-racial impersonation posed to the white performance establishment helped to fuel the new performance mode of blackface minstrelsy.

Who were these black appropriators? I will highlight three individual examples: Richard Crafus, James Hewlett, and Ira Aldridge.[6] The old adage is true once again—truth is stranger than fiction! Richard Crafus (1791?–1831, b. Maryland?) was an American sailor who was captured by the British Admiralty in the War of 1812 and was sent to Dartmoor Prison in Devonshire, England in October 1814. The prison, which was built in 1809, was organized into seven equal-sized buildings. While the prison was not at first segregated, the white American prisoners objected to having to live with blacks. So the Dartmoor officials made "No. 4 the black's prison," and Crafus became the unofficial king of Number Four.

Standing at about 6'3" (when the average height for men at the time was 5'6"), Crafus was nicknamed King Dick and Big Dick. Three memoirs written by white American prisoners of war contain similar descriptions of Crafus. One claims, "These blacks have a ruler among them whom they call *king DICK*. He is by far the largest, and I suspect the strongest man in the prison . . . If any of his men are dirty, drunken, or grossly negligent, he threatens them with a beating; and if they are saucy, they are sure to receive one."[7] Another remarks, "This prison is almost entirely under the control of yonder Ethiopian giant, of six feet seven inches . . . 'Big Dick.'"[8] And the third declares, "A tall, powerful back man, known among the prisoners as 'Big Dick' or 'King Dick'

. . . was nearly seven feet tall and proportionally large, was of a muscular and athletic make, of a commanding aspect, shrewd of mind, and an expert boxer."[9] The historian Jeffrey Bolster argues that, "Under his rule, African Americans organized, disciplined, and entertained themselves, but did nothing to discourage white inmates from visiting the black enclave as customers."[10]

In fact, Number Four became famous both inside and outside the prison for the entertainments hosted there. One white prisoner wrote, "I have spent considerable of my time [in No. 4], for in the 3rd story or Cock loft they have reading whiting Fenceing, Boxing Dancing & many other schools which is very diverting to a young Person, indeed there is more amusement in this Prisson than in all the rest of them."[11] The amusement that interests me the most, however, is the performance of Shakespeare in whiteface.

The prisoners in the different prison buildings at Dartmoor began to compete to see who could draw the largest paying crowd for their performances. Bolster explains, "French prisoners had produced regular plays at Dartmoor 'with very elegant scenery' and 'appropriate comic and tragic dresses.' African Americans purchased sets, props, make-up, and costumes from the departing French, modifying them for their own productions. Meanwhile, an all-white dramatic company in Number Five composed of prisoners and Irish guards competed with the blacks' troupe. Weekly or twice-weekly performances in Number Four cost viewers six pence (four pence for seats in the rear) and included . . . the central attraction—Shakespeare."[12] The performances of Shakespeare at Number Four flourished with the black prisoners playing to packed houses.

The memoirs written by white American prisoners of war discuss these all-black productions and for the most part praise the black prisoners in Number Four for their skill and ingenuity. Yet, one reserves harsh words for a production of *Romeo and Juliet* in Number Four. He notes, "The female parts were played, as they were in London in the early days of drama, by boys; and with their appropriate dresses, and being properly painted, they did the thing well enough. The only exception I ever noticed was in No. 4, where I witnessed a tall, strapping negro, over six feet high, painted white, murdering the part of Juliet to the Romeo of another tall dark-skin."[13] It is unclear why the white prisoner, Benjamin Frederick Brown, thought that the black actor was "murdering the part of Juliet," but the white paint that the actor wore seemed to spark his derision. Male actors playing female parts was a part of performance history, according to Brown, but a black actor in whiteface playing Juliet seemed one step too far for him.

Whiteface impersonation in the service of performing William Shakespeare's plays, in fact, unites all three of the black Proteans I will discuss. The next, James Hewlett (1790?–1850?, b. Long Island or The West Indies?) became the leading actor at the African Theatre in New York.[14] William A. Brown (1780?–1830?), a black West Indian (we think), worked as a steward on transatlantic passenger ships and amassed enough money to become an entrepreneur in New York, opening the first pleasure garden for people of color in August 1821 (located on 38 Thomas Street).[15] Since Brown had experience traveling to the UK, he may have heard about the highly lucrative performances by the black prisoners in Number Four in the Dartmoor Prison. A month after he opened the pleasure garden, Brown staged a production of *Richard III* with an all-black cast, and by October 1821 there were announcements for benefit performances of *Richard III* for James Hewlett, the new star of the company. Hewlett had also been a steward on transatlantic passenger ships, and it is thought that he saw Shakespearean performances in England during his visits there. He seems to have had first-hand knowledge about specific English performers whom he must have seen in the UK.[16] And he readily announced his performances as being in the style of, or in imitation of, Edmund Kean, the most popular Shakespearean actor at the time (Figure 4.2).

While it was commonplace for Shakespearean actors to announce themselves as imitating Kean, for a black actor to do so was exceptional and proved to be offensive to the white establishment. Hewlett was mocked in the press for aping white behavior; his costume was torn off of him when white gangs stormed the African Theatre during a Shakespeare performance; and he was the supposed inspiration for Charles Mathews's "black tragedian (the Kentucky Roscius)" in *A Trip to America*. Like the hyperbolic rhetoric in the white prisoner's assessment that the "painted"

HEWLETT, NEGRO ACTOR, AS RICHARD III

FIGURE 4.2 The black American actor James Hewlett explicitly styled his Shakespeare performances on the white English actor Edmund Kean. The Folger Shakespeare Library (CC by 4.0).

Juliet was "murdering" the part in Dartmoor's Number Four production, the attacks on Hewlett seem to stem from the fact that he dared to white up in Shakespeare.

You have to admire Hewlett, though, because he was no shrinking violet. He published a rebuke to Mathews in a New York newspaper declaring that Shakespeare belonged to everyone. Hewlett made it clear that he knew Mathews had "ridiculed our *African Theatre in Mercer-street*, and burlesqued me with the rest of the negroe actors, as you are pleased to call us—mimicked our styles—imitated our dialects," and asked, "Was this well for a brother actor?" And then Hewlett wrote:

> Why these reflections on our color, my dear Matthews [*sic*], so unworthy your genius and humanity, your justice and generosity? Our immortal bard says, (and he is *our* bard as well as yours, for we are all descendants of the Plantagenets, the white and red rose;) our bard Shakespeare makes sweet Desdemona say,
> "I say Othello's *visage* in his mind."
> Now when you were ridiculing the "chief black tragedian," and burlesquing the "real negro melody," was it my "mind," or my "visage," which should have made an impression on you?[17]

This letter was published in 1824! To put things in perspective: slavery was still legal in New York (it was abolished in 1827); the Civil War was more than three decades away; and John Quincy Adams was about to be elected president (and he would go on to write the 1836 essay, "The Character of Desdemona," which argued that Desdemona deserved to die because she was at fault for race mixing!). It is remarkable to read these words of black assertion, which employed Shakespeare to vocalize his equality.

One more thing about Hewlett: he made a trip to England to confront Mathews in October 1824. Hewlett performed in London and Liverpool late in 1824, and Mathews wrote a letter to his wife claiming that Hewlett was looking for him![18] That's one uppity negro! But Hewlett was not allowed to remain uppity. After the closing of the African Theatre, Hewlett toured parts of the United States and even went to the West Indies to perform. But he never achieved financial security or critical acclaim. In fact, I bet his name is not familiar to many of you.

Ira Aldridge's name (1807–67, b. New York), however, may ring more bells than Hewlett's. He too got his start at the African Theatre in New York, although we do not have any first-hand archival documentation that affirms this. Rather, we know that he filed assault charges against James Bellmont, a white circus performer whose brother led a riot against the black theatre company shortly thereafter (Aldridge was attacked in July 1822, and the riot in the African Theatre occurred a month later in August 1822). Free born and the child of a minister, Aldridge was educated at the African Free School, where he received a classical education. He traveled to the UK in 1825, a year after Hewlett's trip. By October 1825, Aldridge performed in London's Royal Coburg Theatre in scenes from *Oroonoko* and *Othello* (Figure 4.3).

FIGURE 4.3 The black American actor Ira Aldridge frequently employed whiteface. Courtesy Charles Deering McCormick Library of Special Collections and University Archives, Northwestern University Libraries (CC by 4.0).

The reviews were mixed, but Aldridge was not deterred and continued to perform and adapt his persona and techniques. For instance, he claimed to be of African royalty, the Fulani princely line, but by 1831 he was adopting the name F. W. Keene Aldridge, the African Roscius. As I mentioned previously, the English actor Edmund Kean was considered to be the greatest performer of the time, and many white actors readily advertised their performances as being in imitation of his style. Aldridge's adoption of Kean's name, albeit spelled differently, signaled that he too viewed himself in this lineage.

Not content simply to play black roles, Aldridge's repertoire contained many whiteface roles, including Shylock, Richard III, Macbeth, and King Lear (i.e., the most popular Shakespearean roles of the time). While Aldridge's performances were celebrated in eastern Europe, his use of whiteface was derided in the UK. Here is one review from 1857:

> there is a manifest incongruity in a black *Hamlet*, *Macbeth*, *Richard III*, *Shylock*, etc, though the swarthy complexion of the negro is not unsuited to the Moor of Venice, in which part we had the pleasure of seeing Mr. Aldridge on Saturday last. The performance was decidedly original, many parts of it being striking and forcible. As a whole it is uneven, and suffers somewhat by comparison with the highest standards. Often we noticed erroneous emphasis and incorrect reading; but Mr. Aldridge is not to be judged by ordinary rules.[19]

This English reviewer gives voice to the challenges Aldridge faced. It was okay for Aldridge to attempt Othello, although he was assessed to be not as good as white actors, but his attempts to perform white characters showed a "manifest incongruity." White actors in blackface = congruous. Black actors in whiteface = incongruous.

Aldridge had planned to return to the United States after the Civil War, and he hoped his return would be triumphant. He was in the midst of raising the funds when he died in Lodz, Poland in 1867. It is hard to imagine that he would have been greeted with performance laurels in the post-bellum United States. The era that saw the birth of Jim Crow laws might have lynched this uppity negro for applying whiteface.

I have made us linger, looking at black actors in whiteface performances of Shakespeare, because these uppity performances directly challenged the white establishment's explicit biases and implicit performance rules.

- Explicit bias: blacks are inferior to whites.

- Implicit performance rule: blacks are limited— presumably by their inferiority—to exhibiting their bodies for white entertainment.

- Implicit performance rule: the skill and power that are central to performing in general, and to performing other genders and races in particular, are the provenance of white actors' abilities.

Astute and talented black actors like Richard Crafus, James Hewlett, and Ira Aldridge were able to identify and perform the skills and techniques that were valued most in the nineteenth century—namely, an ability to imitate others and to impersonate them through the use of racial prosthetics. After all, white actors had been doing this for at least 200 years to great acclaim.

These astute and talented black actors, however, were not read as being such by the white establishment (i.e., the critics, competitors, and white audiences); rather, they were judged to be "aping" white performance modes. To be accused of aping someone or something is to be accused of mimicking someone else's behavior "pretentiously, irrationally, or absurdly."[20] Aping, like parroting, is assumed to be a thoughtless, mindless, or animalistic imitation without finesse, skill, or even understanding. Imitation reigned supreme on the nineteenth-century stage with white British, Irish, Scottish, American, and even West Indian actors readily imitating each other. They could be white men and white women; they could be black men and black women; they could be East Indian men and East Indian women; they could be American Indian men and American Indian women. And they could do so in various racial prosthetics in imitation of each other's performance techniques (e.g., black versus tawny makeup). As I have previously iterated, to be a black or brown character onstage was to be performed by a white actor in racial prosthetics.

Black actors were excluded from this performance mode because it was at odds with exhibition—the performance mode that blacks had been locked into since at least Shakespeare's time. The legacy of this history is that white actors are often heralded as being virtuosos if they impersonate another gender or race, while it is nearly impossible for black actors to be read as virtuoso performers regardless of what they do.

5 WHAT IS THE LEGACY OF BLACKFACE?

THE IMPACT ON WHITE ACTORS

Returning to the eight-year-old girl who was "Martin Luther King Jr." in blackface at my son's school, I think it is fair to ask what she knew. I'm not asking this to suggest that she knew the nineteenth-century history that I laid out in the previous chapter. While my son knew some of the contours of that history from conversations we had at home, I don't think most eight-year-old kids know that 200-year-old history. Nonetheless, I am not sure that a lack of an awareness of the specifics of that history renders one innocent or inculpable. In fact, I think one of the legacies of blackface is an enduring sense that performing blackness is a white endeavor, and that virtuosity in performance can be tied to cross-racial impersonation. It is not the only way that virtuosity is established, but it is certainly one of the ways that it is established.

But how would an eight-year-old know this, you ask? If she has been exposed to any popular entertainment forms on television, the internet, or the cinema, then she has probably absorbed this legacy passively. I'll highlight three disparate performance modes to show how pervasive blackface was/is in film and television alone. The performances are relatively contemporary, ranging in time from the 1960s to the 2000s. Some have been widely condemned and others profusely heralded. I'm not interested in whether the performances are, or are even considered to be, racist or anti-racist. Rather, I'm interested in showing how often playing black is marked as the domain for white performers. The politics of the performances are less relevant to me than the sustained performance tradition. By all appearances, white people simply love to play black, and they can't give it up even when they know it's wrong. Like a rickroll, white people seem to forever repeat, "Never gonna give you up / Never gonna let you down / Never gonna run around and desert you." Or, perhaps more aptly we should hear their plaintive cry through the most famous line in *Jerry Maguire*: "You complete me."

Blacked Up #1: Late Night Comedy: It would be easy to start a description of blackface in film with a discussion of the first talking film, *The Jazz Singer* (1927), in which Al Jolson blacked up; or to linger on Fred Astaire's blackfaced dance routine in *Swing Time* (1936); or to analyze Judy

Garland's blackface routine in the 1939 film *Babes in Arms*. But I'm doubting that the "Martin Luther King Jr." girl was a fan of 75-year-old films. Her grandparents and parents may have been raised on these performances, but she probably was not. If one were to list the blackface performances in terms of the frequency with which they are rebroadcast, then the 1954 classic film *White Christmas* must win. In that film, Bing Crosby, Danny Kaye, and Rosemary Clooney perform in a large ensemble number that is called the "Minstrel Number," and they even employ the crooked knee dance moves made famous by T. D. Rice's Jim Crow routine. But racial prosthetics were not employed in *White Christmas*— the actors were white while they sing, dance, and tell "black" minstrel jokes. I'm guessing the eight-year-old girl, even if she was exposed to this film every Christmas, might not have understood that specific reference.

So, let's start in the twenty-first century with comedy on television. Apparently, it is too fun and funny to resist blacking up. As I write this, Jimmy Fallon is apologizing profusely for doing a 2000 *Saturday Night Live* skit in which he impersonated Chris Rock in blackface. Despite the fact that NBC had removed the bit from its official website, black Twitter revealed the entirety of the one-minute sketch. In it, "Chris Rock" makes a surprise visit to "Regis Philbin" on his morning talk show, and "Rock" discusses "Philbin's" new hit game show, "Who Wants to be a Millionaire?" Wearing a black leather jacket with a black turtleneck underneath, Fallon dons a short black afro wig and fake goatee, and his hands and face are blackened. While Fallon is clearly attempting to imitate Rock's vocal register, speech patterns, and hand gestures, the skit ends with him looking directly into the camera in an exaggerated smile/snarl that is all too familiar as a minstrel blackface expression (broad, big, and larger than life).

The humor of the sketch seems to be aimed at mocking Philbin, a white septuagenarian (in 2000 when the sketch was made), whom "Rock" jokes has to wake up at "7am to fake laugh at some cruise ship stories." Likewise, "Rock's" jokes about Philbin's game show point out how white the industry is and why it (and by implication Philbin) is not attractive to a diverse audience. That's great material for a pointed comedy sketch about the whiteness of daytime television. But the jokes were delivered in blackface, leaving one to wonder who the butt of the joke really was! Fallon's "Chris Rock" is made to seem both too cool for daytime and too stupid to realize that he is the real joke. After all, "Rock's" jokes traffic in old and tired stereotypes about black people being uneducated and senselessly dandified. *Oh! Hush!* . . .

While Jimmy Fallon has always had a squeaky clean, guy-next-door image, his late-night talk show competitor, Jimmy Kimmel, has not. He's always been the bad boy who was a lot edgier. So, it was slightly less surprising that blackface played a recurring role on his Comedy Central show, *The Man Show*. In a 2001 sketch, Kimmel appeared as "Oprah Jimfrey," who was running in place on top of her Hispanic maid to soften the impact on her knees. In blackface and cross-dressed in a fat suit, Kimmel appeared to be satirizing Oprah Winfrey's mean-spirited privilege and narcissism. But once again the employment of blackface also tapped into an older humor that derides black women for putting on airs and thinking that they are equal to white women (god forbid!). Meet the twenty-first-century dandizette.

Yet Kimmel's recurring blackface performances as the professional basketball player, Karl Malone, showed no light between his performance and the blackface minstrelsy tradition. Here is a transcript from one skit called "Karl Malone on Aliens":

Sometime at night, Karl Malone look at sky and say, what the hell going on up there? Do UFO live on other planet, phoning home like E.T.? Karl Malone read on TV about white people getting deducted by alien. Sticking all kind of hell up they butt, and that's a damn thing. Now, Karl Malone hever seen no flying saucer himself, but if he do, that's gonna be a spooky time. That's why Karl Malone say government got to step up and give 102% to keeping them little green men off this here earth. Cause the day them dudes stick something up Karl Malone butt, that, well, that ain't gonna be a good time for nobody, especially Karl Malone butt. Listen up E.T., you best stay the hell back. Na-nu, na-nu. Until next time, this here Karl Malone.[1]

In the first segment on the show in blackface, Kimmel explained that Karl Malone was his favorite basketball player and that he loved his "philosophical mind." While the Yoda-like grammar may seem to signal a philosophical mind, the "Karl Malone on Aliens" sketch does not present Malone as knowledgeable, wise, or even informed. Rather, he is a malaprop ("deducted by aliens") who is buffoonishly asking the US government to save his butt from alien probes. Can't you see the love in that? Can you feel it? Don't you want to be loved that way?

Because comedians inspire each other, Sarah Silverman had to black up as well! How could she let the guys have all the fun? A former writer for *SNL* (1993–4), Silverman made a name for herself by performing edgy comedy that often addressed taboo topics, like religion, racism, sexism, and even bedwetting. *The Sarah Silverman Program* started on Comedy Central in 2007, and in the first season Silverman included a sketch in which she argued with a black man that it was harder to be Jewish than it was to be black. "Oh, I'm so sorry that you guys had to have great singing voices and really catchy songs, while we got—oh yeah—murder showers." In the end, though, she agrees to try to be black for a day. After visiting a makeup artist, whom the audience assumes is going to make her look authentically black, she appears in stereotypical blackface minstrel makeup. Silverman, cluelessly looking at her blackface in the mirror, celebrated, "I look like the beautiful Queen Latifah" (Figure 5.1).

The sketch was designed to highlight Silverman's obtuseness, but once again the joke had multiple barbs, aiming in multiple directions. And one of them was pointed

FIGURE 5.1 It's not just the men on late night, though. In 2007, Sarah Silverman wore blackface on *The Sarah Silverman Program*. Screenshot.

directly at blackness. Who was the butt of the joke when Silverman declared that she looked like Queen Latifah? Silverman for confusing blackface with an actual black person? Queen Latifah for acting like a minstrel character? Or the idea that black is ever beautiful? All in all, I was left wondering—not unlike Jimmy Fallon's portrayal of Chris Rock—why these were Sarah Silverman's jokes to tell.

Silverman apologized and said that she regretted having done the sketch at all. She also revealed that she was fired from a film after her blackface segment aired. Yet, our next late-night comedian has been celebrated for his blackface portrayals of Barack Obama. Fred Armisen started portraying Barack Obama on *SNL* in 2011. Some critics have attempted to differentiate and distance Armisen's portrayal of President Obama from blackface and blackface minstrelsy because the portrayal did not appear to mock the president. I differ from this view because, as I said from the beginning of this chapter, I am less interested in the politics of any one portrayal than in the sheer volume and continuity of them. I'll label Armisen's blackface (without the minstrelsy part), but the performance still rendered blackness as a performance property that is owned by whites.

To be a black character on a late-night show produced in the United States is probably to be a blackface performance by a white comedian. In fact, I would venture to guess that the number of blackface performances between 2000 and 2020 on late-night shows at least equals, if not outstrips, the number of black comedians employed by them. So, yes, Armisen's performance as Barack Obama did not traffic in the same racist minstrel jokes, but it did traffic in the same racist performance tradition—that performing blackness is the performance property of whites.

I'll simply wrap up this section by noting that Kenan Thompson, a black comedian on *SNL*, did a hilarious sketch in February 2019 in which he portrayed the chair of the ethics committee in the state of Virginia. In an ethics meeting, he is attempting to determine if any other elected officials had dressed in blackface at any point in the past. While the white elected officials ask repeated questions about when it is okay to wear blackface ("What if the blackface was just part of your costume of a black person?" "Does it count if you did it all the way back in the '80s?" "What if you wore the blackface as a tribute, like an homage to your hero?"), they seem not to get that "it was never funny or cool." Finally, Thompson gets increasingly annoyed and says, "No! No more blackface!" It's too bad that he couldn't have said that to his colleagues on late-night shows in general.

Blacked Up #2: Shakespeare: Maybe the "Martin Luther King Jr." girl was not allowed to watch late-night television (although I will protest that eight-, nine-, and ten-year- olds have an uncanny familiarity with the jokes and materials from the shows), but certainly that was not the only way to be exposed to blackface in popular media in the early 2000s. There are more traditional and serious blackface performances, like those in films based on Shakespeare's plays. And while I doubt a third grader would intentionally watch Shakespeare on television of their own volition, sometimes they click through shows long enough to absorb some of it. And if *Othello* is on, there are great opportunities for blackface! The three *Othello* film versions that get aired with the greatest frequency are the 1995 version directed by Oliver Parker and starring the black American actor Laurence Fishburne, the 1965 version directed by Stuart Burge and starring Laurence Olivier in blackface, and the 1981 version directed by Jonathan Miller and starring Anthony Hopkins in blackface.

I'll begin with Olivier's performance because it garnered several academy awards but was nonetheless controversial even at the time of its release. The production originated as a stage play that ran from 1964 to 1965 at the National Theatre in London (directed by John Dexter). When preparing to play the role, Olivier said that he decided to style his performance on the recent West Indian immigrants to the UK, the Windrush generation who arrived between 1948 and 1973. Thus, he covered his entire body in heavy black makeup, adopted a different gait, and even lowered the timbre of his voice significantly to embody his Othello.

In his book *On Acting*, Olivier describes how he developed Othello's walk, voice, and mannerisms first. But he ends by describing his attention to creating Othello's color: "Black all over my body, Max Factor 2880, then a lighter brown, then Negro Number 2, a stronger brown. Brown on black to give a rich mahogany. Then the great trick: that glorious half yard of chiffon with which I polished myself all over until I shone . . . The lips blueberry, the tight curled wig, the white of the eyes, whiter than ever, and the black, black sheen that covered my flesh and bones, glistening in the dressing-room lights."[2] The rhetoric employed should sound familiar. Olivier experienced both pride and pleasure in his full-body transformation. It was a full-scale racial impersonation. And the film encourages to viewer to luxuriate in the pleasure of the impersonation. Olivier's costumes get smaller and smaller as the film progresses, exposing more and more of his painted body and inviting the viewer to wonder how far up the makeup goes. All. The. Way. (Figure 5.2).

Released precisely at the birth of the Black Arts Movement in the United States, the artistic incarnation of the Civil

FIGURE 5.2 Laurence Olivier performed as Othello in blackface in the 1965 film version directed by Stuart Burge. Screenshot.

Rights Movement and the Black Power Movement, one might expect that the film would disappear quietly into the filmic netherworld. But that was not the case—all the principals of the film received Academy Award nominations. While critics in the UK were largely laudatory, critics in the United States were incredulous. There was a sense that Olivier's performance mode crossed several uncomfortable lines. Writing in the *New York Times*, Bosley Crowther bemoaned:

> He plays Othello in blackface! That's right, blackface—not the dark-brown stain that even the most daring white actors do not nowadays wish to go beyond. . . . The

consequence is that he hits one—the sensitive American, anyhow—with the by-now outrageous impression of a theatrical Negro stereotype. He does not look like a Negro (if that's what he's aiming to make the Moor)—not even a West Indian chieftain, which some of the London critics likened him to. He looks like a Rastus or an end man in an American minstrel show. You almost wait for him to whip a banjo out from his flowing, white garments or start banging a tambourine.[3]

Another American critic noted, "I was certainly in tune with the gentleman sitting next to me who kept asking, 'When does he sing Mammy?'"[4] For American critics, then, Olivier's performance mode was too close to the blackface minstrel show tradition in which white actors impersonated black characters and denigrated black identity. Nonetheless, this film and Olivier's minstrel-inflected performance remained in heavy rotation on television and was frequently used as a teaching aid in schools (this was my personal experience in school—yup . . .).

If the 1965 film version accidentally ended up as a popular teaching tool, the 1981 BBC film version, directed by Jonathan Miller and starring Anthony Hopkins, was explicitly designed to be used as a teaching aid. *The BBC Television Shakespeare* project was a seven-year, multimillion-dollar venture that aimed to create film versions of all of Shakespeare's plays that would be aired on television, sold as VHS tapes (eventually DVDs), and distributed globally. This was to be another

British invasion—Shakespeare available for everyone in every corner of the world.

Because of the proposed scale, the budget ballooned, and the British-ness of the production became threatened. When the BBC sought US investors, British Equity, the union for British actors, tried to protect the major roles for British actors. The creator of the series originally wanted the black American actor, James Earl Jones, to play Othello because of his "ability and eminence," but British Equity fought back, arguing that the producers "were overlooking capable black British actors."[5] In order to avoid making the conflict large, the production of *Othello* was pushed back by a year. Susan Willis explains, "The problem was for a time subverted rather than resolved by postponing *Othello* to a later season, though subversion proved to be resolution once Jonathan Miller got hold of *Othello* and decided it was not a play about race at all so did not cast a black actor of any nationality in the role."[6]

Oddly, though, despite the fact that Miller had decided that *Othello* was not a play about race, he still employed racial prosthetics on the Welsh actor Anthony Hopkins. There was a fad in the nineteenth century to have the white actors who were playing Othello wear lighter makeup. This stemmed from the racist and sexist assumption that a white Venetian woman like Desdemona could not fall in love with a "veritable negro" (those are Samuel Taylor Coleridge's words, by the way).[7] Therefore, Othello had to a be light-skinned "Moor." Some have jokingly called this the great "Bronze Age of Othello," the period in which Othello was portrayed

FIGURE 5.3 Anthony Hopkins performed as Othello in blackface in the 1981 *The BBC Television Shakespeare* (dir. Jonathan Miller). Screenshot.

as tanned, tawny, and off-white but definitively non-black.[8] Edmund Kean, one of the most famous Shakespearean actors of the era, was the first to stage the new, lighter-skinned Othello (Figure 5.3).

Miller was clearly tapping into this performance history, but Hopkins looked visually odd. While his makeup was light, it was clearly darker than his normal skin tone, and his very light blue eyes were not covered in brown contact lenses but were rimmed with deep kohl eyeliner. To top things off, Hopkins wore a large wild wig that resembled something akin to Beethoven's unkempt mane. All in all, Hopkins looked like an actor in makeup and a wig—in racial prosthetics. While this might be an interesting art direction if it were intended to draw attention to the artifice of Othello's character, that was not Miller's intention. Rather, Miller wanted his film to counteract the "myth of the performance overwhelming the text."[9] But once again, it announced itself as a production in which the performance of racial, ethnic, and religious differences is white property. And once again, this BBC film was widely advertised, distributed, and used in classrooms across the world. Blackface for all!

Blacked Up #3, or, Ben Stiller's Road to *Tropic Thunder*: In January 2020, Robert Downey Jr. reflected on his decision to play Kirk Lazarus, an Australian method actor who was known to go to extremes to inhabit a character, in Ben Stiller's 2008 parodic film *Tropic Thunder*. In light of the recent blackface scandals that had rocked public figures like Megyn Kelly, Justin Trudeau, and Ralph Northam, Downey was asked to reflect on his decision to play Lazarus. In the film, Lazarus was so committed to playing a black American soldier that he underwent a radical "pigmentation alteration" process that darkened his skin, and he refused to break character—meaning he remained in blackface and black-speak—for the majority of the film. As reported in the *Washington Post*, Downey hesitated only for a moment before accepting the role: "I thought: 'Hold on, dude. Get real here. Where is your heart?' he said earlier this month. 'My heart is a) I get to be black for a summer in my mind, so there's something in it for me. The other thing is I get to hold up to nature the insane, self-involved hypocrisy of artists and what they think they're allowed to do on occasion.'"[10]

I'll come back to Downey's reflections in a moment, but I want to pause to ask a question. How is it possible that a film released in 2008 not only featured a blackface performance, but also was celebrated for that performance? Downey was nominated for best supporting actor awards by the Academy of Motion Pictures, the Golden Globes, BAFTA, the Screen Actors Guild, and the Critics' Choice Awards. Although he did not win any (Heath Ledger won them all posthumously for his performance in *The Dark Knight*), the industry clearly liked Downey's performance. Why? Four reasons:

- A belief in white innocence.
- A belief that performing blackness is white property.
- A belief that virtuosity in acting can be expressed through cross-racial impersonations.
- And Ben Stiller.

I've already addressed the first three in previous chapters of this book, so let's tackle the last.

Ben Stiller is the child of comedians, and he grew up studying, learning, and copying their trade. Stiller got his start performing in children's theatre, doing small parts in television and film, and then by making his own mockumentaries. He has written, directed, and starred in numerous films whose humor is often based on mocking characters for their blithe lack of self-awareness. The 2001 film, *Zoolander*, which Stiller wrote, directed, and starred in, offered a classic example. The film followed Derek Zoolander, a famous male model, who was duped into participating in an international conspiracy to assassinate the Malaysian leader because he threatened to end child labor in garment factories. While good hearted, Zoolander was extremely slow and dim witted.

Zoolander's mental slowness seemed to be the justification for a brief use of blackface in the film. Disheartened that he has lost a modeling award to his rival, Zoolander returned to the coal mines of "southern New Jersey" (!). He found his father and brothers on their way into the mine, and he asked to join them: "All the Zoolander men together again, like when we were kids." Once in the mine with his family and fellow miners, Zoolander strutted in like he was walking the catwalk, struck various modeling poses, and pouted as he lifted small bits of coal. Then, incongruously, he jumped out of the shadows in full blackface and shouted, "Surprise!" to startle his father, who fell down and asked, "What the hell's the matter with you?" (Figure 5.4).

Why does blackface sneak into this scene? Is it simply that film depictions of coal mining inevitably necessitate the blackening of white skin? Are filmic depictions of coal mining the only times when white people can be seen in blackface without being accused of being racist?

I'm not sure, but I think the moment breaks the fourth wall. The audience is temporarily allowed to think about the artifice of the medium. We are allowed to remember that we are watching a film that is by definition an artificial construction. And in that moment, we can ask whether the

FIGURE 5.4 Ben Stiller's character Derek Zoolander appears in blackface while working in the coal mines of southern New Jersey in his 2001 film. Screenshot.

medium and jokes within it are going too far. Like Zoolander's father, we can ask "What the hell's the matter with you?" And Zoolander's response (Figure 5.5) perfectly captured white innocence. He was an innocent who was too stupid to know what was wrong with the joke he had just told.

With Stiller's 2008 film, *Tropic Thunder*, the use of blackface moved from a momentary joke to an entire plot arc. Openly satirizing an espousal of white innocence, *Tropic Thunder* presented an actor whose drive for authenticity saw him staying in blackface for the majority of the film—despite the fact that his black colleague told him that it is offensive. Thus, the notion that performing blackness is white property was satirized in *Tropic Thunder* (Figure 5.6).

The film also seems to satirize the notion that a white actor's virtuosity can be demonstrated through a

FIGURE 5.5 Ben Stiller's character Derek Zoolander embodies white innocence perfectly. Screenshot.

FIGURE 5.6 Robert Downey, Jr. as the Australian actor Kirk Lazarus in blackface in Ben Stiller's 2008 film *Tropic Thunder*. Downey was nominated for every major acting award for this role. Screenshot.

blackface portrayal. After all, Downey's character, Lazarus, annoyingly dispenses acting craft advice to his colleagues, ad nauseum: "the scene is about emotionality, where is it?!" The joke seems to be that only a self-absorbed white actor would assume that he could portray a black character better than a black one. And this was certainly what Downey indicated was one of his reasons for doing the part: "I get to hold up to nature the insane, self-involved hypocrisy of artists and what they think they're allowed to do on occasion."

But isn't that exactly what the industry applauded in Downey's performance? Wasn't his performance lauded for being virtuosic? Didn't blackface grease the wheels for his virtuosity to be made visible? How else can we explain his five nominations for best supporting actor from the most prestigious awarding agencies in film?

The *Washington Post* notes that "In past interviews, Downey emphasized that his character differed from more egregious portrayals of blackface. 'At the end of the day, it's always about how well you commit to the character,' he told *Entertainment Weekly* in 2008. 'I dove in with both feet. If I didn't feel it was morally sound, or that it would be easily misinterpreted that I'm just C. Thomas Howell in [the 1986 movie 'Soul Man'], I would've stayed home.'" Reflecting back on his performance, Downey stated, "Ninety percent of my black friends were like, 'Dude, that was great.'" And acknowledging that some black critics raised serious concerns, he added: "I can't disagree with them, but I know where my heart was. It's never an excuse to do something that is out of place and not of its time, but to me it was just putting . . . a blasting cap on."

I can't help but interpret Downey's comments from both 2008 and 2020 as appealing to the things the film purportedly satirized:

- White Innocence: "I know where my heart was."
- White Virtuosity: "At the end of the day, it's always about how well you commit to the character."

This leaves the performance of blackness firmly rooted as white property. And this leaves the employment of blackface in American popular culture stunningly pervasive. Sadly, there were too many opportunities for the little girl who blacked up to be "Martin Luther King Jr." to see the performance of blackness as a white property on both big and small screens. I'll simply add that I did not have to delve into the horrors of the uses of blackface on the internet to make this case. There were ample opportunities for "Martin Luther King Jr." to witness—repeatedly—claims to the white ownership of blackness in film and television alone.

6 WHAT IS THE LEGACY OF BLACKFACE?

THE IMPACT ON BLACK ACTORS

Of course, the little white girl who was "Martin Luther King Jr." was not the only child watching the abundance of blackface performances on the big and small screens at the turn of the millennium. Children of color, like my son, were watching too, and this chapter thinks through some of the implications for their consumption of this recurring media trope. And again, I'd like to ask: why didn't my son and the other few children of color at his private elementary school apply whiteface to be their white heroes? If the white kids thought that they needed to blacken up to fully embody their chosen idols, then why didn't the children of color feel the same need for embodiment, racial verisimilitude, and/

or authenticity? The answers stem in part from the complex performance legacy of 1) who has the authority to determine the authenticity and veracity black performances, and 2) what performance modes are available for black actors.

As I have repeated throughout this volume, the performance of blackness was marked as a white property from the beginning of English performance history. But what does this actually mean? After all, there are lots of black actors who have become famous for playing black characters—Ruby Dee, Sidney Poitier, Diahann Carroll, Billie Dee Williams, Cicely Tyson, Morgan Freeman, Viola Davis, and Denzel Washington are just a few who come to mind immediately. Obviously, I am not suggesting that there are no black actors who play black characters, but rather that playing black is a complicated performance endeavor. To be clear, playing white is also a white property, but that makes it a decidedly less complicated performance endeavor for white actors. White actors do not describe their acting challenges in terms of authenticity.

To recap: In Shakespeare's lifetime, blackness was performed in two modes—exhibition (black people on display) and imitation (white men in racial prosthetics). Because in the exhibition mode all the power resided in the viewer (not the one exhibited), and because in the imitation mode all the power resided in the white, blacked up performer, performances of blackness were a white performance property for actors and audiences. In the nineteenth century, blackness and whiteness were performed by black actors for the first time in the United States and the United Kingdom, and their performances challenged the long-standing assumptions that (1) blackness was a white performance property and (2) only white actors could be virtuoso performers. These early nineteenth-century black performers were denigrated by white critics, white audiences, and their fellow white actors for "aping" white performance modes. The criticisms these black actors faced told them to stay in their lane, a lane which indicated they were only fit for imitation and "aping."

In the twenty-first century, it is possible to see the legacy of these unequal horizons of expectations for black performers in three distinct performance modes: minstrelsy/ imitation, exhibition/trauma, and anxiety/authenticity. As with the examples analyzed in the previous chapter about the legacy of blackface minstrelsy for white performers, I am not necessarily interested in asking or answering if any of these performances are racist or anti-racist. In many ways, what these examples demonstrate is that the 200-year-old performance tradition of blackface minstrelsy lingers within black performances today, and it impacts the black children who watch these performances as well.

Performance Mode #1 Minstrelsy/Imitation: Tyler Perry began writing plays in the 1990s that were focused on the struggles of working-class black Americans. They often had a melodramatic structure with explicitly redemptive Christian endings. Writing in the *New York Times Magazine*, Wesley Morris described Perry's plays as "loud, long, hysterical shows in which a bunch of characters, not infrequently on a set resembling a sitcom diorama, love and leave one another, imparting morals the way a shot gets put. They aren't quite farces, dramas or melodramas. They're not exactly parables, musicals or church, either. They're usually all of those things. Somebody's mad, somebody's cheating, somebody's dying, somebody's scheming. Here's some dirt. Here's some slapstick. Here's a gospel song. Here's the truth. Oh, Lord."[1]

Although not immediately successful, Perry's plays grossed enough money touring on the urban theatre circuit between 1999 and 2005 that he was able to finance his first film, *The Diary of a Mad Black Woman* (2005) to the tune of $5M, and it went on to gross over $50M. The film, which was based on Perry's 2001 play, is about:

Helen, a woman who has discovered that her "perfect" marriage is falling apart. After literally being thrown out of her house by her husband and his new mistress, Helen returns to her small hometown and turns to her Aunt Madea for a place to stay. In the film writer/director comedian Tyler Perry portrays Mabel "Madea" Simmons, a fictional character he created. Madea is an aggressive, grey-haired, Black woman behaving as a matriarch, who according to Perry, is based on his mother and aunt. She often argues with others on issues such as relationships, the bible, and any family concern. She often threatens people by pulling a gun out of her purse, and she has a tendency for malapropisms as reflected in interpretation of the bible stating, "Peace be still" as "my piece be steel" (referring to her gun).[2]

Perry has donned his special cross-dressed fat suit to play Madea in twelve films to date (the latest in 2019). Many of the Madea films have grossed over $25M each, making Perry one of the most successful writer/director/producers in Hollywood. In fact, in 2011 Forbes listed him as the highest paid man in entertainment for earning $130M the previous year (Figure 6.1).

To be clear, Perry's Madea films are black written, black funded, black produced, black performed, and black directed. They are black artistic creations that were, at least initially when produced for the stage, pieces designed for

FIGURE 6.1 Tyler Perry's Madea employs "fat-suit minstrelsy" in his 2005 film *The Diary of a Mad Black Woman*. Screenshot.

black audiences. Nonetheless, the Madea films borrow heavily from the mammy stereotype that was birthed in the white-created and white-performed blackface minstrel shows of the nineteenth century. Spike Lee has pointedly criticized Perry's films for being "coonery and buffoonery," or artistic creations that rely on minstrelsy's stereotypical character types like the Tom, the Coon, the Mammy, and the Buck.[3] Baruti N. Kopano and Jared A. Ball explain that "The mammy of American popular culture and film is a mythical creation who is the antithesis of the idealized notion of American womanhood."[4] Mammy is obese, dark, aggressive, loud, and often irrational. They continue, "Despite many American men seeing large breasts and prominent buttocks as desirable physical traits for women, the mammy stereotype exaggerates these features so much so as to make them sexually undesirable, yet maternally nurturing."[5]

While many white comedians have cross-dressed on film—think for example of Tony Curtis and Jack Lemmon in *Some Like It Hot* (1959), Dustin Hoffman in *Tootsie* (1982), and Robin Williams in *Mrs. Doubtfire* (1993)—bell hooks has argued that black male cross-dressing taps into slightly different socio-cultural registers. In a "heterosexist cultural gaze," hooks argues, the men who cross-dress cross "over from a realm of power into a realm of powerlessness."[6] When black men cross-dress, however, they may be opting to swap one racist stereotype for a different racist/sexist stereotype. hooks explains:

it is not surprising that many black comedians appearing on television screens for the first time included as part of their acts impersonations of black women. The black woman depicted was usually held up as an object of ridicule, scorn, hatred (represented the "female" image everyone was allowed to laugh at and show contempt for). Often the moment when a black male comedian appeared in drag was the most successful segment of a given comedian's act (for example, Flip Wilson, Redd Foxx, or Eddie Murphy).

I used to wonder if the sexual stereotype of black men as overly sexual, manly, as "rapists," allowed black males to cross the gendered boundary more easily than white men without having to fear that they would be seen as possibly gay or transvestite. As a young black female, I found these images to be disempowering. They seemed to both allow black males to give public expression to a general misogyny, as well as to a more specific hatred and contempt toward black women.[7]

In terms of Tyler Perry's cross-dressed performances of Madea, Iliana De Larkin argues that he bolstered a new form of minstrelsy, "fat-suit minstrelsy," which serves to "perpetuate the beliefs that large Black women are asexual, emasculating, domineering, and most of all, not to be taken seriously."[8]

Perry has countered critiques like these by arguing that they are "insulting" to his "fan base." He argues, "It's attitudes like that that make Hollywood think that these people do not exist, and that is why there is no material speaking to them, speaking to us."[9] What does it mean if "speaking to us" involves employing old racist, sexist stereotypes that were created by white performers 200 years prior? And does the answer to this question change if we take into account the fact that the films were huge financial successes? Does that change our estimation of whether they were "speaking to us" or about us behind our backs, or worse, to our faces?

I'll circle back to these questions a bit later in the chapter, but for now I want to linger on the fact that Perry is not unique in employing this performance mode. As bell hooks first explained, and as Iliana De Larkin elaborated, there is a long history of black men cross-dressing in fat suits to denigrate black femininity and maternity: Flip Wilson, Redd Foxx, Eddie Murphy, Martin Lawrence, and Tyler Perry are just the first names that come to mind, but there are many, many more. What I want to emphasize is that the imitative performance mode—one in which black actors borrow from white-created minstrel performance tropes—has a long tradition. It is an established and acceptable mode for black actors to perform blackness, and it is founded on racist and sexist principles.

Performance Mode #2 Exhibition/Trauma: While the comedic, cross-dressing, imitation mode for performing blackness is often rewarded financially, the exhibition/trauma mode for performing blackness is often rewarded by the film industry itself. The Academy of Motion Picture

Arts and Sciences, the Screen Actors Guild, and other award-granting agencies most frequently reward films "about" black Americans when the films are actually about their great, white American saviors (*The Blind Side*, *Amistad*, and *The Green Mile*). Black actors are also rewarded for performing black roles that clearly help white characters find and/or restore their mojo (Oscars went to Whoopie Goldberg in *Ghost*, Cuba Gooding Jr. in *Jerry Maguire*, and Morgan Freeman in *Million Dollar Baby*). And sometimes black actors are rewarded if black trauma is fully embodied in their performances (Oscars went to Halle Berry in *Monster's Ball*, Mo'Nique in *Precious*, and Lupita Nyong'o in *12 Years a Slave*).

I'm going to focus on this last category because it is a clear descendent of the 400-year-old exhibition mode of performing blackness. And like Tyler Perry's Madea films, I'd like to focus on a black written and black directed film, *12 Years a Slave* (2013), because I am interested in the legacies and lasting impacts of minstrelsy on black creators in this chapter of the book. As I said before, it is not simply white children, performers, writers, directors, producers, and audiences who have absorbed the lessons of minstrelsy; it is also black children, performers, writers, directors, producers, and audiences too. And in this exhibition/trauma mode of performing blackness, we are all collectively absorbing "repetitive images of abused Black Bodies. Scarred Black Bodies. Chained Black Bodies pressed together on ships, on wagons, on floors—longing to fulfill the desire for freedom

FIGURE 6.2 Chiwetel Ejiofor's excoriated black body in the 2013 film *12 Years a Slave*. The audience is invited to witness his trauma. Screenshot.

and to shield themselves from certain pain. Excoriated Black Bodies . . ."[10] (Figure 6.2).

The 2013 film *12 Years a Slave* was based on the 1853 narrative of enslavement by Solomon Northrup. Northrup, who was a freeman living in New York, was kidnapped by traders when he was in Washington, DC in 1841, and he was sold as an enslaved person to a series of enslavers in Louisiana for the next twelve years. When he was released, he wrote his memoir to help with the efforts of the abolitionist movement. The black British director Steven McQueen wanted to direct a film about slavery in the United States, and he recruited the black American writer John Ridley to help him develop a script. It wasn't until they read *Twelve Years a Slave* that they saw a way forward. Adapting Northrup's memoir, they had the perspective they both wanted—a tale about the realities of the horrors of slavery written from an enslaved person's perspective.

While McQueen was already a lauded director, his previous films had never addressed race, anti-black racism, or even American characters. The writer John Ridley, however, had spent his entire career tackling race, racism, and representations of race in the media in his creations. The challenges of representing the brutality of slavery and the challenges of representing a true black American subjectivity in the face of harshly sadistic circumstances were precisely what McQueen and Ridley hoped to address. In other words, they knew the potential pitfalls.

Part of their strategy was to rely on the veracity of the source text. Jasmine Nichole Cobb argues, "Producers associated with *12 Years* make sure to rehearse proofs of the film's validity as part of the promotion."[11] They even went so far to hire Henry Louis Gates Jr. as an "historical consultant on the film and [he] provided the second major signifier of accurateness. Gates is renowned as an African-American studies scholar, with publications on nineteenth-century African-American literature . . . "[12] As Cobb argues, though, this adherence to validity also led McQueen to highlight the violence perpetuated on the black bodies of the enslaved:

"On screen, the presence of violence is the key trope that signifies *12 Years* as a legitimate portrayal of slavery. McQueen is emphatic about the brutality of the peculiar institution."[13]

The film's unwavering focus on the brutality has led many to question the overall impact of watching *12 Years*. Valerie Smith notes about a long scene depicting Northrup hanging from a tree, "The unbearably long take requires viewers to watch the scene of Northrup's torment and to be aware of our status as spectators. Ironically, we are also drawn into the scene by its very beauty . . . Through his use of these elements, Steve McQueen asks us to look long beyond the point at which we would prefer to avert our eyes and to be distracted by the next plot twist."[14] Nonetheless, this type of scene setup and camera work are also typical of "mainstream cinematic tropes structured by the sadomasochistic gaze. McQueen's film actively relies upon tropes of mastery and domination, pain and trauma . . ."[15]

This has led some to feel that McQueen's film is trafficking in "torture porn." For instance, Armond White, a black film critic, argued, "*12 Years a Slave* belongs to the torture porn genre with *Hostel*, *The Human Centipede* and the *Saw* franchise."[16] While I too found the violence in *12 Years* nauseating, I would not place the film in the same generic line with the *Saw* franchise. Rather, I see it in line with Renaissance exhibitions of black bodies. It is hard for me to watch the film and think that it is intended for a black viewer, and that stems from my understanding of how the cinematic gaze works. Stephanie Li articulates it well when she argues:

> Laura Mulvey contends that the cinematic apparatus is structured to replicate the point of view of the active male and implicitly white, heterosexual subject while woman functions as the passive object of this gaze. Though McQueen structures the film through Northrup's perspective, his positioning of the male protagonist as passive wreaks havoc with the gender politics of the gaze. McQueen may be understood as reifying the racial politics of the gaze by subjecting suffering male and female black bodies to the gaze of his camera. However, these images continually emphasize Northrup's powerlessness, and as filtered through his perspective, they act less as a kind of fetishistic display than as a sign of his impotence.[17]

In other words, even though the film aims to give voice to Northrup by positioning him as the center of the narrative through whom the audience experiences the events, his powerlessness in the face of unbridled sadistic acts by the white enslavers renders him an impotent figure. That status as the figure whose voice is powerless but whose body is nonetheless always available for the white gaze is exactly the performance mode—exhibition—that the Renaissance audience enjoyed.

Black writer, black producer, black director, and all-star black cast who helped to shape the arc of the film and

12 Years a Slave ends up back in a representation mode that was established in seventeenth-century England. That's a trip . . .

Of course, *12 Years a Slave* is not unique. This is a problem that has literally 400 years of history. As bell hooks warns, Americans live in a society that "has deemed black folks more body than mind. Such thinking lies at the core of all the stereotypes of blackness (many of which are embraced by black people) . . ."[18] What's to be done? As Carol Henderson points out, "The question then becomes, How does one disrupt those processes that mold the social meanings of the black body? What are the ways in which one can restructure those social discourses that are built on this body as sign/language? How does one regain agency in a system intent on destroying one's motive will?"[19] These are precisely the questions the creators of the next mode ask. Astute consumers of the imitators and exhibitionists, the authenticity creators grew up in African American literature, history, culture, and theory classes. They can quote from critical race theory fluidly, and they worry about how to produce an authentic performance of blackness.

Performance Mode #3 Anxiety/Authenticity: There is no evidence to suggest that the black actors in the nineteenth century who were applying whiteface to perform as Juliet, Macbeth, Shylock, King Lear, and other white characters worried about authenticity. Learning from their white counterparts that performance was an imitative form that crossed races and genders, they seemed to approach performance as an appropriative endeavor. As I argued in chapter four, this uppity stance is precisely what angered and enraged their white critics. Nineteenth-century black actors had to be taught that performance was a white property, including the performance of blackness.

In the 2000s, however, this lesson has been fully absorbed by black performers, especially on television. There has been a rash of shows whose black characters obsessively worry about the authenticity of their portrayals of blackness, and once again these shows are by and large written, produced, and directed by black artists. Examples include portions of *The Dave Chappell Show*, *Insecure*, and *Twenties*. I will focus on Kenya Barris's sitcom *#blackAF* because Barris's insecurities about his authenticity play a major role throughout the first season (at the time of writing this book there has only been one season).

Kenya Barris is a native of Los Angeles, and he graduated from Clark Atlanta University, an historically black university in Atlanta, Georgia. Almost immediately upon graduating, Barris began working in Hollywood as a writer for television. He cut his teeth writing for black-themed shows like *The Keenen Ivory Wayans Show*, *Soul Food*, *Girlfriends*, and *The Game*. He was one of the creators of the Tyra Banks reality show, *America's Next Top Model*, and he wrote the screenplays for *Girls Trip* and *Shaft*. Barris's superstar status, however, was earned because of the hit show, *black-ish*, for which he was the creator, writer, and executive producer. *black-ish* spawned two spin-off shows, *mixed-ish* and *grown-ish*, and

#blackAF is not so much a spin-off as a meta-show about a man named "Kenya Barris" who wrote a hit television show called "black-ish."

The title of the show plays on the saying "black as fuck," which Doreen St. Felix deconstructs beautifully:

> Think of the hashtag #blackAF as a millennial remix of mantras of self-love—"Black is beautiful," "I'm black and I'm proud." The phrase, printed on T-shirts and stamped on skin, has become a kind of shorthand for a politics of affirmation. But does it also veil a prickly insecurity? "Black as fuck" is the kind of thing an artist or a businessman might say about his work or his behavior in order to foreclose critique. After all, who is anyone to question anyone else's blackness? Employed earnestly, the phrase makes people wary: Why the fuck do you feel that you have to proclaim your blackness? On the other hand: Why the fuck is it such a big deal to you if I do?[20]

The last two questions that St. Felix poses reside precisely in the heart of Barris's show. Moreover, because the show is so self-aware of the limits of black performance, it is also cognizant of the traps that the imitators and exhibitionists have fallen into even—or perhaps most *especially*—when they are rewarded for doing so.

Treated in a semi-satirical fashion, the show tackles the legacy of slavery in almost every episode. In fact, the eight episodes are called: "because of slavery," "because of slavery too," "still . . . because of slavery," "yup, you guessed it. again, this is because of slavery," "yo, between you and me . . . this is because of slavery," "hard to believe, but still because of slavery," "i know this is going to sound crazy . . . but this, too, is because of slavery," and "i know you may not get this, but the reason we deserve a vacation is . . . because of slavery." While the episode titles are intended to be humorous by poking fun at "Barris's" never-ending authenticity woes, the show nevertheless traffics in a type of edutainment—with voiced-over bits about African American history.

For instance, the first episode of *#blackAF* revolves around "Kenya's" large gold chain that he has worn for years. He wonders if he needs to alter or tone down his "flexing" in front of white people. He worries about the power and impact of the "white gaze" on his behavior, most especially his dress: "I don't want to be super-duper fly every day. This is what I have been forced into. They're turning me into a peacock." When his white assistant asks how he has turned "Kenya" into a peacock, the show launches into an actual mini-documentary about what happened to former enslaved persons during the reconstruction era. Accompanied by black and white archival photos from the late nineteenth and twentieth centuries and Nina Simone's 1967 song "I Want a Little Sugar in My Bowl," the one-minute documentary visually and aurally presents a history of the African American belief that "presentation equals acceptance"[21] (Figure 6.3).

Borrowing a page from Monica Miller's scholarly work on the roots, meanings, and legacy of black dandyism,

FIGURE 6.3 Kenya Barris's *#blackAF* demonstrates the authenticity blues through the show's inclusion of edutainment moments. Screenshot.

#blackAF connects structural racism to seemingly minor acts by its characters.[22] Yet as Doreen St. Felix argues, the satirical tone of the show renders these connections unstable at times:

> Barris is responding, in part, to the curdling of the Zeitgeist since the Obama era, a period in which any art that seemed to analyze the performance of blackness was immediately deemed resonant. On each episode of *black-ish*, Barris used a trademark monologue to link a character's personal crisis to structural racism. In *#blackAF*, he parodies the speciousness of that device. "Being dripped is literally part of who we are," Kenya says, unironically invoking slavery to justify his Mr. Porter addiction.[23]

The show presents the structural issues unironically—the establishment of the white gaze through the legacy of white enslavers dressing their enslaved persons in their best clothes for church to demonstrate the white enslavers' beneficence to other white enslavers—but presents the current impact ironically: "Kenya's" declaration that his addiction to $2,000 track suits is epigenetic.

Again, the show seems informed by and steeped in the theories of African American cultural criticism, especially with regard to the elusive nature of black authenticity. E. Patrick Johnson's brilliant book, *Appropriating Blackness: Performance and the Politics of Authenticity*, seems to establish the terms of the show's tensions:

> Blackness, too, is slippery—ever beyond the reach of one's grasp. Once you think you have a hold on it, it transforms into something else and travels in another direction. Its elusiveness does not preclude one from trying to fix it, to pin it down, however—for the pursuit of authenticity is inevitably an emotional and moral one . . . Often, it is during times of crisis (social, cultural, or political) when the authenticity of older versions of blackness is called into question. These crises set the stage for "acting out" identity politics, occasions when those excluded from the parameters of blackness invent their own.[24]

#blackAF can articulate the problems with claims of authenticity, but it cannot necessarily resolve them. Who can

after all? What the show does demonstrate, though, is that the modes of performing blackness that rely on imitation—like Tyler Perry's Madea films, and/or trauma/exhibition like Steve McQueen's *12 Years a Slave*—have just as little of a claim to authenticity as his show. Black authenticity does not exist, just as white authenticity does not either (unless you are a white supremacist).

What does this mean exactly? It means that black children, like my son, who watched television and movies in the 2000s have seen a strange range of performances of blackness. On the one hand, they have seen Tyler Perry make hundreds of millions of dollars in fat-suit minstrel performances of blackness. Imitating blackness = financial success. On the other hand, they have seen Steve McQueen and John Ridley win prestigious awards for exhibiting the horrors wracked on black bodies in an exhibitionist fashion. Exhibiting blackness = awards. And then they have seen Kenya Barris question the entire notion of an authentic performance of blackness. In the end, as disparate as these performance modes are, they all leave one with the sense that performing blackness is still a white property that uneasily sits on black bodies.

Now I don't want to suggest that there are no other performances of blackness that were available or imaginable in the 2000s. And I'm painfully aware that my "performance history" is oddly gendered male. There are other options, and black women have often created them. I am thinking of Tiffany Haddish's performance in *Girls Trip* as one powerful example of a black character type that had not been fully explored before—a zany, un-self-conscious black woman. The legacies of performances of blackness—the idea that performing blackness is a white property—had precisely no impact on Haddish's character. Her character did not know about a white gaze, and that was exactly why she seemed to burst off the screen in more technicolor than her castmates (Figure 6.4).

Haddish's exception, though, does seem to prove the rule. There was a woeful lack of diversity in the performances of blackness on big and small screens even when black writers, producers, and directors controlled the content. If performing blackness offered such a contested ground, then

FIGURE 6.4 This is what freedom looks like, Tiffany Haddish in the 2017 film *Girls Trip*. Screenshot.

I don't think that black children can make the leap that they can embody, inhabit, or imitate another race. The lesson that black children are shown most often is that performance is a fraught ground. They are taught that authenticity is elusive. They see that there are limits on personal and even cultural expressions. These lessons do not open oneself to the possibility of claiming ownership, or even borrowing privileges, to performing another race. In fact, they do just the opposite. These examples discourage performing other identities whatsoever. No wonder, then, that the handful of children of color in my son's third-grade class did not whiten up to embody their white heroes.

7 CONCLUSION

I CAN'T BREATHE

In the middle of writing this book George Floyd, an unarmed 46-year-old black man, was killed on the street in Minneapolis by a white police officer, Derek Chauvin, who knelt on his neck for eight minutes and forty-six seconds. Floyd, who was handcuffed and lying face down on the pavement, repeatedly told the officer, "Please, I can't breathe," and called out to his departed mother. Despite the fact that Floyd was motionless, silent, and non-responsive after five minutes on the ground, and despite the fact that brave onlookers begged the police officers to at the very least check his pulse, Chauvin continued to kneel on Floyd's neck until paramedics dragged his lifeless body onto a stretcher. When the stretcher was rolled into the ambulance, Floyd was still handcuffed even though he had no pulse.

The brutality and senselessness of Floyd's killing has stunned the world, and protests in both large and small cities have sprung up in the United States, United Kingdom,

France, Canada, Italy, Iran, and many other countries. There is a renewed interest in the Black Lives Matter movement fueled by a thirst for change, for systemic change, and for informed dialogues about race, racism, and the specific contours of anti-black racism. Many of the protestors involved are young white people, members of Generation Z.

It is hard to describe the depth of the pain and trauma that Floyd's killing has inspired in many, including me. Any black scholar who works on racism becomes adept at compartmentalizing their research so as to be able to stay sane, but I could not keep the damage and the suffering in a neat little box in the aftermath of Floyd's killing. And I could not pretend that there was no relationship between the topic of this book and the way those officers treated George Floyd. There is a filthy and vile thread—sometimes it's tied into a noose—that connects the first performances of blackness on English stages, the birth of blackface minstrelsy, contemporary performances of blackness, and anti-black racism. Yes, there are important differences between the years 1520, 1820, and 2020, but there are also ties that continue to bind and to make me feel that I can't breathe.

One of the ties is this sense that performing blackness is still a white property. In the midst of the protests against anti-black racism, several white influencers posted Instagram images of themselves as black—in black makeup—in what they intended to be performances of solidarity. The posts were mainly from Eastern European and Middle Eastern women, and they believed they were expressing support for blacks around the world. One was posted by the Lebanese vocalist Tania Saleh who was "sporting a photoshopped Angela Davis-esque Afro and black skin paint. The photo was captioned 'wish I was black, today more than ever . . . Sending my love and full support to the people who demand equality and justice for all races anywhere in the world.'"[1] The Algerian artist Souhila Ben Lachhab posted a photo of herself with half her body painted brown. Her post stated: "Just because we're black on the outside, doesn't mean we're black on the inside," she wrote unironically. "Racist people are the true black heart ones. They are black on the inside, and they know it"[2] (Figure 7.1). 1520, 1820, 2020—how

FIGURE 7.1 White influencers on social media attempt to show their solidarity with the Black Lives Matter movement by applying blackface. Twitter.

much distance is there when these posts are performances of solidarity, support, and a belief that black lives matter?

No, these photos were not created by American, English, or Canadian influencers, but does that matter? Blackface minstrelsy was exported to the Middle East, Eastern Europe, the Far East, and much of the rest of the world in the nineteenth and twentieth centuries. For instance, blackface performances continue to be mounted with regularity in Japan, but it was Americans who introduced the performance tradition to them. In 1854, Commodore Matthew C. Perry arrived in Japan with "An Ethiopian Entertainment," a blackface minstrel show, as a central part of his "solidarity" plans for the United States with the newly opened Japan.[3] This is just one example of the invasive spread of blackface performances from the United States and the United Kingdom to the rest of the world. So, the influencers in the Middle East and Eastern Europe who painted their faces black to support the Black Lives Matter movement were not doing so in a vacuum. Blackface minstrelsy had a performance history in their countries as well, but like the principal at my son's elementary school these women had never needed to absorb this history before.

Equally disturbing, there are white artists who have absorbed the performance history of blackface and have then attempted to appropriate the symbols of that history as a way to signal that their creations are edgy and transgressive. The fashion industry has done exactly this recently. For instance, in its Fall/Winter 2018 line, Gucci debuted a black wool

Balaclava knit top black
by Gucci
$890

Select a Size

🛒 Sold Out

Product details

Style 548540 X1688 1125
The Fall-Winter 2018 runway show space reflected the stark
environment of an operating room, emulating the theme of...

Show more

Free shipping & returns

About the brand

FIGURE 7.2 Gucci's Fall/Winter 2018 line featured this edgy turtleneck that creates a minstrel face for the wearer. Gucci's website.

turtleneck for $890 that rolled up to cover one's nose and mouth, but the mouth hole featured large, red minstrel-style lips (Figure 7.2). As the Associated Press reported, "Luxury fashion is all about breaking codes, creating a new, irresistible message that captivates consumers. But some of the globe's top brands have raised eyebrows with designs that have seemingly racist undertones. The latest instance of that was Italian fashion designer Gucci . . . Its similarity to blackface prompted an instant backlash from the public and forced the company to apologize publicly on Wednesday. Gucci also withdrew the offending garment from sale on websites and stores."[4]

Similarly, in 2016, the French luxury fashion house Moncler released a winter coat that featured blackface minstrelsy's caricatured smiley face as part of the design (Figure 7.3).

FIGURE 7.3 In 2016, the French fashion house Moncler released a winter coat that accidentally featured a minstrel face. Moncler's website.

Although the "Malfi" line was suspended, Moncler's apology will sound familiar—it relies on the logic and rhetoric of white innocence. The apology posted on Twitter states in part: "We are deeply troubled if the face, seen out of its context, could be associated with past or present unacceptable, racially offensive caricatures. This could not have been further from our thinking and we unreservedly apologise for any distress this may have caused" (Figure 7.4).

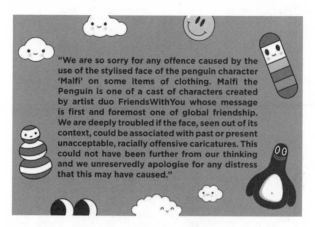

FIGURE 7.4 Moncler's apology on Twitter: white innocence. Twitter.

Moncler is "deeply troubled" because their designers did not intend to cause offense. Would it have mattered if there was someone at Moncler who could have alerted them to the offensive nature of the design? While many critics asserted that the problem highlights why design houses need to hire designers of color, the next example puts pressure on the idea that advance warnings will be heeded by their white "edgy" colleagues.

In February 2020 a Fashion Institute of Technology (FIT) student fashion show included a line that featured large prosthetic lips and monkey ears as fashion accessories (Figure 7.5). As reported in the *New York Times*, "The controversy began when Amy Lefevre, a 25-year-old model,

FIGURE 7.5 In 2020, the FIT student fashion show featured accessories that resembled minstrel imagery. When alerted to this problem ahead of time, the professionals involved in producing the event said it would not read as "racially ignorant." Really? "Fashion Institute of Technology's Fine Art Of Fashion And Technology Show," Bennet Raglin/Getty Images for FIT.

refused to wear the accessories, which she said had been given to the models just as they were about to walk out for the show. 'I let the staff know that I did not want to wear these pieces as they were clearly racist and made me incredibly uncomfortable,' she said in an interview on Sunday. Other models wore the pieces. Mr. Huang [the student designer] would have let her walk without them, she said, but the director of the show, Richard Thornn, a creative director of NAMESldn, a London-based fashion agency, yelled at student designers to move away and pressured her to wear the accessories. She said Mr. Thornn told her that she'd 'only be uncomfortable for 45 seconds.' But she refused."[5] Other student designers indicated that they too had raised concerns about the accessories ahead of the show. One reported, "'My concerns were laughed off,' he said. 'They said that in the right context it won't read as racially ignorant.'"[6] Of course, this example reveals as much about the power structures in the fashion industry and its reckless disregard for the models employed as it does about the legacy of blackface minstrelsy, but the two are not unrelated. The same imbalances of power enable one to declare that it is okay to force someone to be "uncomfortable for 45 seconds" and to appropriate minstrelsy's performance tropes for fashion.

The idea that an appropriation of racist iconography and/or racist performance traditions will not be read as "racially ignorant" is finally being fully questioned by white artists. Just this week Tina Fey, the creator and executive producer of the sitcom *30 Rock*, announced that four episodes of the show that featured blackface are now removed from the platforms that stream the show; *30 Rock* ran from 2006 to 2013 and was a satire of a live comedy late-night sketch show, like *SNL*. In letter to the streaming services, Fey explained, "As we strive to do the work and do better in regard to race in America, we believe that these episodes featuring actors in race-changing makeup are best taken out of circulation . . . I understand now that 'intent' is not a free pass for white people to use these images. I apologize for pain they have caused. Going forward, no comedy-loving kid needs to stumble on these tropes and be stung by their ugliness. I thank NBC Universal for honoring this request."[7]

The four episodes that included blackface performances are: season three's "Believe in the Stars"; season five's "The Live Show" and "Christmas Attack Zone"; and season six's "Live from Studio 6H." To be clear, these episodes were all created, filmed, and aired when Barack Obama was the forty-fourth president of the United States. Nicholas Sammond's 2015 book, *Birth of an Industry*, made the connection between Fey's "edgy" race humor and President Obama's election painfully clear. Sammond argues, "the wink and nod moment following the election of an African American president . . . somehow generated permission for media producers to more freely express racist stereotypes and sentiments under the dictum that a forthright acknowledgment of racism also provides for its ironic absolution . . ."[8] After the killing of George Floyd, Fey no longer felt the cover of an "ironic absolution" and decided that no one—especially children like my son and the girl who was "Martin Luther King Jr."—should have to stumble innocently on the "fun" of blackface.

Another sign that white artists are understanding that racialized performances should no longer be their property comes with the announcement that *The Simpsons* will no longer allow white actors to voice the characters of non-white characters. After thirty-one years on the air (!), the creators have said that "Moving forward, *The Simpsons* will no longer have white actors voice nonwhite characters."[9] While Hank Azaria's voicing of the Indian immigrant, Apu, has garnered a lot of criticism over the years, there are several other characters of color on *The Simpsons* who are voiced by white actors, "including Homer Simpson's workmate, Carl Carlson, (played by Azaria) and the Simpson family physician, Dr. Hibbert (played by Harry Shearer)."[10]

Similarly, the hit animated show *Family Guy* will cease to have a black character voiced by a white actor. As reported in the *New York Times*, "Mike Henry, a *Family Guy* voice actor who is white, said in a tweet that he would no longer play the role of Cleveland Brown, a black character who has appeared on that series since its debut in 1999. 'It's been an honor to play Cleveland on *Family Guy* for 20 years,' Henry wrote in his tweet. 'I love this character, but persons of color should play characters of color. Therefore, I will be stepping down from the role.'"[11] Likewise, Kristen Bell and Jenny Slate, two white actresses who voice bi-racial characters on separate animated shows, have indicated that they intend to stop doing so as well. After the killing of George Floyd, white artists have started to acknowledge that performing blackness should not be a white property, regardless of their intentions—love, satire, or comedy in general.

I have framed this book through an examination of the employment of blackface to perform black heroes by white children at my son's elementary school in 2012. After the litany of examples that fill the pages of this book—from *SNL* to *30 Rock* to *Othello*, from Ben Stiller to Sarah Silverman to Sir Anthony Hopkins—it is no wonder that those children thought it was normal, appropriate, and expected to embody blackness through a blackface imitation. And it is no wonder that those children thought that an application of blackface was a demonstration of love and genuine respect. Up until this current moment, white people have believed that performing blackness was a white property that could—if done with the proper intent—demonstrate, physically, one's love of black identity and culture. Of course, this assumption rests on the white supremacist belief that white innocence trumps all, including a violently racist history.

I have also framed this book by asking why the black and brown children who chose white heroes for their school assignment did *not* employ whiteface. On the most basic level, there is no litany of examples of whiteface performances crowding their screens. While there are very specific appropriations of whiteface by comic actors including Eddie Murphy, the Wayans brothers, and more recently Maya Rudolph (as Donatella Versace on *SNL*), there is no overwhelming performance tradition of black and brown people crossing over to play white. This would require a very different historical arc.

Let me conclude with one last example. In 2019 to 2020 my daughter, Thaisa, was in fourth grade in a public school in Arizona. Since the social studies standards had recently changed in the state, all of the students in her grade were required to participate in "Colonial Day" as part of their early American history unit. The teachers were focusing on "European settlements" of the Americas and required each student to dress as a "colonial," even suggesting costumes that could be made or purchased. In their costumes, the students would be doing "colonial" activities like churning butter and making cornhusk dolls. When my daughter showed me the assignment sheet, I was a bit incredulous. Did the teachers really want the children to dress as colonizers? This, after all, is in Arizona, and there are Native American students in my daughter's class. Did they want them to dress as the colonizers who forcibly removed them from their ancestral lands? All of this seemed not well thought through. And, in fact, the social studies teachers with whom I spoke acknowledged as much. They indicated "Colonial Day" was merely meant to be a fun way to get through this bit of the curriculum.

There was more to my uneasiness about the instructions for "Colonial Day," though, that I couldn't quite articulate to the teachers. I did not want my brown daughter to dress as white at anyone else's request. If she chose to be Martha Washington or Paul Revere on her own, I would find and buy the cutest colonial outfits available. I would enable her to rock her "Paul Revere" identity to the best of my abilities. And let me emphasize unequivocally that I LOVE the sixteenth, seventeenth, and eighteenth centuries. I'm a Shakespeare scholar, and I have spent my entire career studying this exact time period. I have nothing against teaching, learning, studying, and becoming absorbed in the history of the colonial era—it's a truly fascinating historical period. But I could not stomach the idea that white teachers were requiring my brown child to play a white—even for one day. This uneasiness, I think, stems from a history that denigrates black and brownness and renders whiteness as the aspirational goal.

Yet, I think the teachers in my daughter's school were channeling a different performance history all together. It took me a while to realize that they may have been attempting to channel the popularity of the 2015 Broadway hit musical, *Hamilton*. Written by Lin-Manuel Miranda, *Hamilton* is a musical narrative about the founding fathers, and the cast was (and continues to be) comprised almost entirely of actors of color. If I were to guess, I would say that the teachers who conceived of "Colonial Day" may have been attempting to channel the "fun" of playing founding fathers from *Hamilton*. Many fans of the show believe that the cast was selected in a colorblind fashion, that is with no regard for the races of the actors in a meritocratic fashion— the best part going to the best actor. This was simply not the case for *Hamilton* though; this is a fundamental misreading of the production.

When an ad to re-cast *Hamilton* was announced in 2016 encouraging "non-white" actors to audition, a New York city lawyer objected saying that it was discriminatory. The producers of the show, however, made it clear that they would not back down, stating: "It is essential to the storytelling of *Hamilton* that the principal roles, which were written for nonwhite characters (excepting King George), be performed by nonwhite actors."[12] Writing in the *Atlantic*, one critic noted, "The episode highlights just how intentional, and arguably radical, *Hamilton*'s makeup is."[13] Miranda was incredibly intentional about the way the cast would look racially; it was no accident.

The intentionality of Miranda's casting gives me hope that there may be a new historical arc forming for performance. There are a lot of new playwrights of color who are experimenting with performance traditions and challenging the notion that anything is a white property. Playwrights like Branden Jacob-Jenkins, Mfoniso Udofia, David Henry Hwang, and others readily challenge old performance modes. I am also cheered by the fact that many of these playwrights have been snatched up by television to create new content for the bevy of streaming providers like Netflix and Amazon that are now creating content.

But I am also sobered by the fact that racial representations looked like they had to change in the wake of the Black Arts Movement in the 1960s and 1970s. So much beautiful, empowering, and challenging work came out of that movement, and it has positively impacted black artists in the decades since. Its impact on white mainstream art, however, is negligible. Was Tina Fey aware of the Black Arts Movement when she wrote the four episodes of *30 Rock* that contained blackface in the 2000s? Yes. Did it stop her? No. Why? Because there is a more powerful historical arc that has reaffirmed over and over again that performing blackness is a white property.

Yet, I will end on a note of cautious optimism. George Floyd's killing has made a difference. People want to engage in new, more informed dialogues about race. In the past thirty years there have been numerous books on blackface minstrelsy, and many of the arguments presented in this book have been rehearsed by others. My hope is that this book is more accessible, understandable, and clear about the costs of blackface performances. And my hope is that in this particular historical moment, after George Floyd's killing in 2020, readers can absorb this performance history in a new way, a way that inspires change.

I hope the teachers in my children's schools will read this book and reflect on their teaching practices. I hope the parents of my children's classmates will read this and reflect on the lessons they teach at home. I hope artists like Tina Fey, Ben Stiller, Tyler Perry, and Kenya Barris will read this and reflect on the art they make. I hope that artists who are still in school will read this and create new performance modes. But honestly, my greatest hope is that this will be the last book we will ever need on blackface. The arc toward justice may be long, but performance arcs do not need to be. To quote Kenan Thompson's brilliant 2019 *SNL* skit, "No! No more blackface!"

NOTES

Chapter 2

1 *Megyn Kelly Today*, season 2, episode 212, October 23, 2018. The segment can be seen on YouTube: https://www.youtube.com/watch?v=VY1Hf2taOPY.

2 Quoted in Sara M. Moniuszko, "Megyn Kelly apologizes for blackface comments on *Today*, gets ripped by Don Lemon," *USA Today*, October 23, 2018, https://www.usatoday.com/story/life/entertainthis/2018/10/23/megyn-kelly-slammed-blackface-comments-today-show/1738580002/.

3 Elizabeth Koh, "Secretary of State Mike Ertel resigns after photos of him in blackface surface," *The Miami Herald*, January 24, 2019, https://www.miamiherald.com/news/politics-government/state-politics/article225030145.html.

4 Quoted in Laura Vozzella, Jim Morrison, and Gregory S. Schneider, "Gov. Ralph Northam admits he was in 1984 yearbook photo showing figures in blackface, KKK hood: Northam, a Democrat, apologizes as demands for Republicans and some Democrats demand resignation," *Washington Post*, February 1, 2019, https://www.washingtonpost.com/local/virginia-politics/va-gov-northams-medical-school-yearbook-page-shows-men-in-blackface-kkk-rob

e/2019/02/01/517a43ee-265f-11e9-90cd-dedb0c92dc17_story.
html.

5   The entire 42-minute press conference (February 2, 2019)
can be seen on *The Washington Post*'s website. All citations
to follow come from this video: https://www.washingtonpos
t.com/video/politics/watch-va-gov-northams-full-press-c
onference-amid-yearbook-controversy/2019/02/02/2fabc77
e-0af7-4bb7-b5b4-10aa97cbfa65_video.html.

6   Quoted in Dan Merica, "Virginia attorney general admits
to wearing blackface at 1980 college party," *CNN Politics*,
February 7, 2019, https://www.cnn.com/2019/02/06/politics/
virginia-attorney-general-blackface/index.html.

7   "What we know about Justin Trudeau's blackface photos—
and what happens next," *CBC News*, September 20, 2019,
https://www.cbc.ca/news/politics/canada-votes-2019-trud
eau-blackface-brownface-cbc-explains-1.5290664.

8   Justin Trudeau's press conference, September 18, 2019,
https://time.com/5680759/justin-trudeau-brownface-photo/.

9   The entire September 20, 2019 press conference can be seen
on the CBC website: https://www.cbc.ca/news/politics/ca
nada-votes-2019-trudeau-blackface-brownface-cbc-explains-
1.5290664.

10   Kimberlé Crenshaw, *On Intersectionality: Essential Writings*
(New York: New Press, 2017).

Chapter 3

1   Anthony Gerard Barthelemy, *Black Face, Maligned Race: The
Representation of Blacks in English Drama from Shakespeare*

to Southerne (Baton Rouge: Louisiana State University Press, 1987), 3–4.

2   Jonathan Burton, *Traffic and Turning: Islam and English Drama, 1579–1624* (Newark: University of Delaware Press, 2005), 92; Matthieu A. Chapman, "The Appearance of Blacks on the Early Modern Stage: *Love's Labour's Lost's* African Connections to Court," *Early Theatre* 17-2 (2014): 86.

3   Martin Banham, *The Cambridge Guide to Theatre* (Cambridge: Cambridge University Press, 1995), 919.

4   Quoted in Mrs. Mathews, *The Life and Correspondence of Charles Mathews, The Elder, Comedian* (London: Routledge, Warne, and Routledge, 1860), 284.

5   Ibid., 289.

6   Ibid.

7   Charles Mathews, *Sketches of Mr. Mathews Celebrated trip to America. His Admirable Lecture on Peculiarities, Characters, and Manners. Stories and Adventures, and eight Original Comic Songs. with four elegant engravings* (London, 1824), reprinted in *The Broadview Anthology of Nineteenth-Century British Performance*, ed. Tracy C. Davis (London: Broadview Press, 2012), 190.

8   Quoted in Tracy C. Davis, "Acting Black, 1824: Charles Mathews's *Trip to America*," *Theatre Journal* 63.2 (2011): 177–78.

9   "An Old Actor's Memories: What Mr. Edmon S. Conner Recalls about his Career," *New York Times*, June 5, 1881, 10.

10 Colonel Morris, *The Mirror* (October 5, 1833). Quoted in W. T. Lhamon Jr., *Jump Jim Crow: Lost Plays, Lyrics, and Street Prose of the First Atlantic Popular Culture* (Cambridge: Harvard University Press, 2003), 20.

11 Letter to the editor of the *Mirror*, October 11, 1833. Quoted
    in W. T. Lhamon Jr., *Jump Jim Crow: Lost Plays, Lyrics, and
    Street Prose of the First Atlantic Popular Culture* (Cambridge:
    Harvard University Press, 2003), 22.

Chapter 4

1 Imtiaz Habib, *Black Lives in the English Archives, 1500–1677*
   (Burlington, VT: Ashgate, 2008).

2 Dympna Callaghan, *Shakespeare Without Women:
   Representing Gender and Race on the Early Modern Stage*
   (London and New York: Routledge, 2000), 77.

3 Quoted in Kim F. Hall, *Things of Darkness: Economies of Race
   and Gender in Early Modern England* (Ithaca, NY: Cornell
   University Press, 1995), 23.

4 Thomas Heywood, "Prologue to *The Jew of Malta*" (London,
   1633), A4v.

5 Anonymous, "Funerall Elegye on the Death of the famous
   Actor Richard Burbage who died on Saturday in Lent the
   13 of March 1619."

6 For an entire book on whiteface, see Marvin McAllister,
   *Whiting Up: Whiteface Minstrels and Stage Europeans in
   African American Performance* (Chapel Hill: The University of
   North Carolina Press, 2011).

7 Richard Waterhouse, *A Journal, Of a Young Man of
   Massachusetts* . . . (Boston: Rowe and Harper, 1816),
   174–77.

8 Josiah Cobb, *A Green Hand's First Cruise, Roughed Out from
   the Log-Book of Memory, of Twenty-Five Years Standing:*

Together with a Residence of Five Months in Dartmoor. By a Younker (Boston: Otis, Broaders, and Company, 1841), 43–45.

9   (Benjamin Frederick Brown), Nathaniel Hawthorne, ed. *The Yarn of a Yankee Privateer* (New York: Funk & Wagnalls Company, 1926), 181–86.

10 W. Jeffrey Bolster, *Black Jacks: African American Seaman in the Age of Sail* (Cambridge, MA: Harvard University Press, 1997), 103.

11 Quoted in Bolster, *Black Jacks*, 103.

12 Bolster, *Black Jacks*, 120.

13 (Brown) Hawthorne, *The Yarn of a Yankee Privateer*, 239.

14 Two fabulous resources on Hewlett's life are: George A. Thompson Jr., *A Documentary History of the African Theatre* (Evanston, IL: Northwestern University Press, 1998); and Shane White, *Stories of Freedom in Black New York* (Cambridge, MA: Harvard University Press, 2002).

15 Thompson, *A Documentary History*, 4.

16 Ibid., 9.

17 James Hewlett, *National Advocate* (May 8, 1824).

18 In a letter dated January 1825, Mathews writes, "Hewlet [*sic*] has been here, and gave an 'At Home'" and "to challenge me, for ridiculing him in a part he never played." Mrs. Mathews, *A Continuation of the Memoirs of Charles Mathews . . .* 2 vols (Philadelphia: Lea and Blanchard, 1839), 1: 292.

19 *Morning Star*, October 19, 1857. Cited in Bernth Lindfors, "'Mislike Me Not for My Complexion . . .': Ira Aldridge in Whiteface," *African American Review* 33.2 (1999): 351.

20 "Ape, v." *OED Online*, Oxford University Press, March 2020: www.oed.com/view/Entry/9057.

Chapter 5

1 The transcripts for all the Karl Malone sketches on *The Man Show* can be found on a fan site: http://www.jimmykimmel.net/submissions/karlmalone/.

2 Laurence Olivier, *On Acting* (London: Weidenfeld and Nicolson, 1986), 109.

3 Bosley Crowther, "*Othello* (1965): The Screen: Minstrel Show 'Othello': Radical Makeup Marks Olivier's Interpretation," *New York Times* (February 2, 1966).

4 Chester Higgins, "Othello: Noble Black" *Jet Magazine* (March 17, 1966).

5 Susan Willis, *The BBC Shakespeare Plays: Making the Televised Canon* (Chapel Hill: The University of North Carolina Press, 2002), 14.

6 Ibid.

7 Samuel Taylor Coleridge, "Notes on Some Other Plays of Shakespeare, section IV" (1818) in *Lectures and Notes on Shakespeare and Other English Poets*, volume 1 (London: G. Bell & Sons, 1904), 386.

8 I have not been able to determine who coined the term the "Bronze Age of Othello" because it is often cited and never fully attributed. The earliest reference I have been able to find is from 1969, but even in that instance scare quotes are employed, indicating that the phrase was already in circulation. See Carol Jones Carlisle, *Shakespeare from the Greenroom: Actors' Criticisms of Four Major Tragedies* (Chapel Hill: University of North Carolina Press 1969), 194.

9 Quoted in John J. O'Connor, "TV: Miller Directs *Othello*," *New York Times*, October 12, 1981, C24, https://www.nytimes.

com/1981/10/12/arts/tv-miller-directs-othello.html#:~:text=
Tonight%20at%208%20o'clock,Incurably%20provocative%
2C%20Mr.

10 Allyson Chiu, "Robert Downey Jr. on 'Tropic Thunder'
blackface: '90 percent of my black friends were like, "Dude, that
was great,"' *Washington Post*, January 22, 2020, https://www.
washingtonpost.com/nation/2020/01/22/downey-blackface-
tropic-thunder/.

Chapter 6

1 Wesley Morris, "All His Children," *New York Times Magazine*,
October 13, 2019, 51.

2 Iliana De Larkin, "If the Fat Suit Fits: Fat-Suit Minstrelsy in
Black Comedy Films," in *Interpreting Tyler Perry: Perspectives
on Race, Class, Gender, and Sexuality*, eds. Jamel Santa-Cruz
Bell and Ronald L. Jackson (New York: Taylor & Francis
Group, 2013), 49.

3 Spike Lee quoted in "Our World with Black Enterprise,"
May 31, 2009, https://web.archive.org/web/20100106194319/
http://www.blackenterprise.com/tv-video/our-world/full-ep
isode-our-world-with-black-enterprise-tv-video/2009/05/30/
our-world-episode-73.

4 Baruti N. Kopano and Jared A. Ball, "Tyler Perry and the
Mantan Manifesto: Critical Race Theory and the Performance
of Cinematic Anti-Blackness," in *Interpreting Tyler Perry:
Perspectives on Race, Class, Gender, and Sexuality*, eds. Jamel
Santa-Cruz Bell and Ronald L. Jackson (New York: Taylor &
Francis Group, 2013), 38.

5 Ibid.

6 bell hooks, *Black Looks: Race and Representation* (Boston: South End Press, 1992), 146.

7 Ibid.

8 De Larkin, "If the Fat Suit Fits," 55.

9 Tyler Perry, "He Is One of America's Top Filmmakers, Yet Few Have Ever Heard of Him," *60 Minutes*, October 22, 2009, https://www.cbsnews.com/news/tyler-perrys-amazing-journ ey-to-the-top-22-10-2009/4/.

10 Tara T. Green, "Black Masculinity and Black Women's Bodies: Representations of Black Bodies in *Twelve Years a Slave*," *Palimpsest: A Journal on Women, Gender, and the Black International* 4.1 (2015): 1.

11 Jasmine Nichole Cobb, "Directed by Himself: Steve McQueen's *12 Years a Slave*," *American Literary History* 26.2 (2014): 341.

12 Ibid.

13 Ibid.

14 Valerie Smith, "Black Life in Balance: *12 Years a Slave*," *American Literary History* 26.2 (2014): 363.

15 Rizvana Bradley, "Reinventing Capacity: Black Femininity's Lyrical Surplus, and the Cinematic Limits of *12 Years a Slave*," *Black Camera* 7.1 (2015): 163.

16 Armond White, "Can't Trust It," *City Arts: New York's Review of Culture*, October 16, 2013.

17 Stephanie Li, "*12 Years a Slave* as a Neo-Slave Narrative," *American Literary History* 26.2 (2014): 331n.3.

18 bell hooks, "Feminism Inside: Toward a Black Body Politic," in *Black Male: Representations of Masculinity in Contemporary*

American Art, ed. Thelma Golden (New York: Whitney Museum of Art, 1994), 129.

19 Carol E. Henderson, *Scarring the Black Body: Race and Representation in African American Literature* (Columbia: University of Missouri Press, 2002), 5.

20 Doreen St. Felix, "Black Like Me: *#blackAF*, on Netflix," *New Yorker*, May 4, 2020, 80.

21 Kenya Barris, "because of slavery," *#blackAF*, season 1, episode 1, 2020.

22 Monica Miller, *Slaves to Fashion: Black Dandyism and the Styling of Black Diasporic Identity* (Durham, NC: Duke University Press, 2009).

23 St. Felix, "Black Like Me," 81.

24 E. Patrick Johnson, *Appropriating Blackness: Performance and the Politics of Authenticity* (Durham, NC: Duke University Press, 2003), 2.

Chapter 7

1 Ben Cost, "Instagram influencers spark outrage for donning blackface in support of BLM," *New York Post*, June 11, 2020, https://nypost.com/2020/06/11/influencers-spark-outrage-for-donning-blackface-in-support-of-blm/.

2 Quoted in Cost.

3 William H. Bridges, *Playing in the Shadows: Fictions of Race and Blackness in Postwar Japanese Literature* (Ann Arbor: University of Michigan Press, 2020), 2.

4 "Gucci was selling a blackface sweater for $890 until yesterday," *Associated Press*, February 8, 2019.

5 Kimiko de Freytas-Tamura, "F.I.T. Model Refuses to Wear 'Clearly Racist' Accessories," *New York Times*, February 23, 2020, https://www.nytimes.com/2020/02/23/nyregion/fit-racist-fashion-show.html.

6 Quoted in de Freytas-Tamura.

7 Quoted in Christine Hauser, "Streaming Services Remove '30 Rock' Blackface Episodes," *New York Times*, June 23, 2020, https://www.nytimes.com/2020/06/23/arts/television/30-rock-blackface-Tina-fey.html.

8 Nicholas Sammond, *Birth of an Industry: Blackface Minstrelsy and the Rise of American Animation* (Durham, NC: Duke University Press, 2015), 16.

9 Quoted in Dave Itzkoff, "White Actors Leaving Nonwhite Roles at 'The Simpsons' and 'Family Guy,'" *New York Times*, June 26, 2020, https://www.nytimes.com/2020/06/26/arts/television/family-guy-simpsons-white-voice-actors.html.

10 Ibid.

11 Ibid.

12 Quoted in Spencer Kornhaber, "*Hamilton*: Casting After Colorblindness. A brief controversy over the play's pursuit of diversity reminds just how potent that diversity is," *Atlantic*, March 31, 2016.

13 Ibid.

INDEX

Page references for illustrations appear in *italics*